Seeing Life:
Finding God

To Dave and Myra
With love,

James L. Merrell
June 2006

Seeing Life: Finding God

◆

Vivid Experiences Offer Fresh Insight Into Some Old Words

James L. Merrell

iUniverse, Inc.
New York Lincoln Shanghai

Seeing Life: Finding God
Vivid Experiences Offer Fresh Insight Into Some Old Words

iUniverse books may be ordered through booksellers or by contacting:

iUniverse
2021 Pine Lake Road, Suite 100
Lincoln, NE 68512
www.iuniverse.com
1-800-Authors (1-800-288-4677)

ISBN-13: 978-0-595-39982-6 (pbk)
ISBN-13: 978-0-595-84370-1 (ebk)
ISBN-10: 0-595-39982-7 (pbk)
ISBN-10: 0-595-84370-0 (ebk)

Printed in the United States of America

Contents

Preface vii

CHAPTER 1   Everlasting. 1

CHAPTER 2   The Heart 4

CHAPTER 3   The Rock. 7

CHAPTER 4   Hope. 10

CHAPTER 5   Genuine 13

CHAPTER 6   Faithful 16

CHAPTER 7   Father 19

CHAPTER 8   Mother 22

CHAPTER 9   Age 25

CHAPTER 10   Peace. 28

CHAPTER 11   Teacher 31

CHAPTER 12   Laughter 34

CHAPTER 13   Language. 38

CHAPTER 14   Real. 42

CHAPTER 15   Guide 45

CHAPTER 16   Value. 48

CHAPTER 17   Judgment. 51

CHAPTER 18   Healing 54

CHAPTER 19   Song..................................... 57

CHAPTER 20   Courage.................................. 60

CHAPTER 21   Success.................................. 63

CHAPTER 22   Shelter 66

CHAPTER 23   One 69

CHAPTER 24   More 74

Preface

"But blessed are your eyes, for they see, and your ears, for they hear."

—(Matthew 13:16)

Many privileged men and women before me—and scores still to follow—will have had an opportunity to fulfill their passion for writing through an honest yet "friendly" pursuit of *religious* truth.

As I prepared for a career in journalism I was taught in both high school and college to probe for reliable information and to seek truth wherever it might be found—to be a clear-eyed, open-minded observer of persons, events and trends. A seat at the old roll-top desk once used by famed war correspondent Ernie Pyle (while he also edited the Indiana University student daily) was humbling but also empowering. I saw myself as one who, in some yet-to-be-determined field of communication, might help others also "see" reality, uncover hidden facts, determine what is true or is false, and advance civilization in some small way.

Along the way toward graduation and a job search that would lead to a writing career, perhaps with some newspaper or magazine, I felt myself being pulled toward the field of religious communications. Unanticipated opportunities and enticing challenges came in rapid succession. So it was that I found myself continuing on to seminary and then being drawn deeper and deeper into what was for me a still-mysterious realm generally called *institutional church communications*.

As a child I learned to respect the old saying, "Seeing is believing". (My grandmother expressed that same idea in a Cervantes phrase she modified with Hoosier insight as "The proof's in the pudding.") This was one foundation block of the practical ethical code I learned at home and in school and church. The principle is that it is not enough just to profess belief in some lofty but vague moral and spiritual values. One must demonstrate a commitment to those beliefs through daily actions that others may readily observe. Truth of any kind must be visible in some way in the events and experiences and lessons of everyday life.

As a prospective journalist I knew that a major part of my future responsibility would be that of defending the "consumer" by separating fact from fiction, truth from corporate hype, reality from pretense—assisting others in their own search for what is lasting and worthy. I would, in a way, be the "eyes" for others as they tried to observe what is happening around them, and I would seek to bring fuzzy images of people and events into sharper focus.

"Seeing is believing" became an even more significant principle for me as my career in religious communications lengthened and deepened. The well-understood and respected secular journalist's mission of searching for fact to support ideal remained the same for me as I sought to catalog and interpret trends and events (and conflicts) in the *religious* realm.

What is the *evidence* for God's presence and authority in life now? How are people who profess faith in God *demonstrating* their beliefs in actions that heal, uplift and create?

At times I found myself discouraged and even doubting. In so many instances I wanted to believe and be hopeful but saw so much within the community of faith that mirrored the whole ugly range of human weakness and sin. If "believing" required some frequent sightings of courageous faithfulness to keep it alive, I knew as a religious journalist that much of what I was observing and reporting at the moment would hardly lead the diehard skeptic to make a leap of faith.

But God had more experiences for me as the years moved on and I matured as a journalist and a "proclaimer of the Word" both in print and as a pastor/preacher—and whenever I wondered if humankind truly is worth saving or if there is a bedrock truth on which one may rest confidently, I would meet people who lifted my soul to the heights. Time after time I was thrust into situations where it was obvious to me that God's ongoing handiwork and continuing providential care were beyond question.

This little book is a vehicle for me to look back over the years at the persons who are part of my story and the events and experiences that have come my way through little effort on my part—and then to reaffirm that "seeing *is* believing".

I offer here some stories that I hope readers will recognize as reflections of an exuberance growing out of *confident faith* rather than as examples of personal boasting. In all sincerity, I feel that I have looked at life as a responsible, objective journalist should—and I have found such amazing and abundant evidence of God that this one small book cannot contain it all.

Jesus told his disciples, as Matthew reports it, that their eyes would be "blessed"—their vision would be broadened and sharpened even more—because they had looked at the amazing jigsaw puzzle of life and had seen the larger picture God wanted them to find.

May readers of these random reflections find some small blessing as they ponder the many words used in an attempt to describe the Source of All Things and then see how their own daily experiences bring these concepts to life.

What do *you*, the reader, "see"? Look around. Be a good observer and reporter. I hope you will see, as I have, the face and hand and heart of God.

James L. Merrell

1

Everlasting

*"Lord, you have been our dwelling place in all genera-
tions....from everlasting to everlasting you are God."*
—**(Psalm 90:1, 2b)**

The green-uniformed Russian security officer resembled a wax museum
figure as he stood inside the entryway at attention—jaws clamped tightly
and eyes flickering only just a little as he surveyed the radiant, pungent
scene before him.

Our group of visiting American religious representatives hardly noticed
this lone somber guard after we caught our first glimpse of the magnificent
golden altar and sumptuous icons of the small tsarist chapel nestled inside
the Kremlin.

Our military watchdog, however, took note of the special attention we
were giving to a small, bent old woman in a heavy brown woolen coat.
The woman was busily guiding a small brown-haired boy on an apparently
one-on-one personalized tour of this great venerable Orthodox museum-
church.

The *babushka* ("old woman") looked like nearly all of the other elderly
females we had seen on our fraternal visit to the then-Soviet Union. She
was a seeming clone of millions of cohorts who had survived war and hunger and repression and were to be encountered at every turn—sweeping
gutters, cleaning streets, selling lottery tickets, marketing wooden dolls,
and replacing thin little church tapers with lightning speed just as they
were ready to burn out.

We from the United States watched in fascination as this one *babushka*
pointed her stubby finger emphatically at various panels of a huge icon-

style painting placed near the side altar. Each framed section, we discerned through the haze of candlelight and incense, told of some key incident in the life of Jesus, from birth to ascension.

All at once the immobile military figure at our side came to life. Our government guard looked at the scene unfolding before him and then turned to some of us with what certainly appeared to be a slight "unauthorized" smile.

"This is what you Americans might call a 'Sunday School lesson,'" he said in surprisingly good English.

Then he turned toward the front again and resumed his role as sentinel guarding one of his national treasures.

The *babushka* continued her animated "Sunday School lesson", ignoring the milling tourists all about her who were jabbering in a half-dozen languages. Was the pupil her grandson or perhaps her great-nephew? Could he have been a neighbor's child? We didn't learn the answer but we knew we had that morning in Moscow seen one tiny woman of faith standing up against a self-proclaimed atheistic power. She was making fools of those who might have believed they could keep members of her beloved family circle from learning the story of the Living and Triumphant One in whose honor this gilded chapel was erected centuries before!

God of "*all generations*". Age after age God's reign goes on and on. Timeless. Eternal.

In the mid-1970s, as many North American churches began to worry about the declining presence of younger persons in the pews, one warning hit home to those of us on the front lines of pastoral ministry. We were reminded that the church always is "one generation away from extinction."

Those active church members with children or grandchildren took this as a personal, urgent summons to action. Denominational leaders poured out hundreds of books and study guides and audio-visuals designed to keep younger persons connected with their faith communities. Evangelism was freshly pointed toward "holding" our youth and young adults.

Some of these efforts were productive, but it was the *personal* touch that got results. The "babushka method" was—as always—the best for keeping the young in the church or at least planting within their hearts the seeds of faith that would later blossom.

In every church setting I would continue to see grandmothers and grandfathers and uncles and aunts and neighbors faithfully bringing kids to worship and church school. In many cases, parents themselves were unable or unwilling to do the patient and sometimes thankless job of shepherding. Perhaps work demands were heavy on weekends. Or home unity was fractured by separation, illness or divorce.

It was my own grandmother who one day decided it was time for me to learn about the Bible. So, while my parents worked into the night and slept on Sunday morning, it was she who got me dressed up and walked me five blocks down the street to enroll in Mrs. Mitchell's Sunday School class and sign up for Mrs. Parris' children's choir.

This is often how God's "rule" is maintained and enhanced generation after generation despite every grim prediction and discouraging statistic. God's chief assistant in mission and church growth often looks like that elderly grandmother I met in the Kremlin.

This week, as I have for dozens and dozens of years, I will look around in church and observe the latest corps of very special evangelistic troops sitting in the pews with squirming kids at their side. Arms around each other, a grandparent and grandchild will be reading the day's Bible text or attempting to hit the right note as they join in singing a not-so-familiar hymn of the day. During the sermon, one or both may doze off.

Half a century later, one could come back and see the same scene repeated. Different cast, *surely*. Same scenario, *most certainly*.

"From generation to generation." On and on the story spreads afresh—until God's loving rule is acknowledged in all the earth.

"From everlasting to everlasting...."

2

The Heart

"...for the Lord does not see as mortals see; they look on the outward appearance, but the Lord looks on the heart."

—(1 Samuel 16:7b)

Nearly every seat in the small sanctuary of Torrington Church in Kingston was filled. It was a day of celebration—an anniversary as I recall—and people came from all over the island to be in this historic white block building located in an especially impoverished section of Jamaica's teeming capital city.

I found a small open spot near the center aisle and wedged myself in the pew next to an elderly Jamaican man. He extended a rough hand that perhaps was calloused through years of banana cutting or road grading. His frayed suit, too heavy for the Jamaican summer heat, was in obvious need of a cleaning.

My seat mate welcomed me in his beautiful Caribbean *patois*, commented on the current hurricane probabilities and the ever-dismal island economy—and then quieted as the program participants entered and the musician at the pump organ started the prelude.

I looked around for a Bible so I might follow the opening Scripture reading. My new Jamaican friend, seeing that I had brought no Bible with me, handed me his own dog-eared copy.

"Please keep it," I protested. "You will need it during the service."

The old man broke out in a gold-toothed grin, thumped his chest slightly, and passed his copy to me with the comment: "Don't worry, mon. The words are in me heart. The words are in me heart."

God of the heart—the loving Creator, who possesses a kind and compassionate heart, as Scripture says, and then reaches into our own hearts to change and empower us at the depth of our being.

As a pastor and also at times as a concerned family member, neighbor or friend, I have visited many hospital cardiac units. They always amaze me. Few areas of medicine have made greater advances than that connected with the maintenance, repair and even replacement of the special organ that beats some three million times during an average lifetime.

But the heart also represents something deep within us: the force that drives the human spirit and will and mind.

◆   ◆   ◆

The writer Charles Siebert once reflected on his own bypass surgery and concluded that we cannot treat the human heart as a machine to be tinkered with. He wrote that we must understand what poets, mystics and theologians have said across the ages—that there is something else deep within us that empowers our life. There is the physical heart as an organ but there is another "heart" that cannot be treated so easily in the hospital or the physician's office.

We have seen a heart that breaks…a heart that yearns, one that dreams. I have on my desk one precious heart that graces a crude, hand-painted valentine from my grandson. The word *heart* symbolizes so much.

This is how Jesus presented the complex issue of faith and works. He said that when we "make the tree good" we then will "produce good fruit." We must deal with the inner person before we put too much dependence on laws and regulations and constraints. Living the full, meaningful life is a blessed "affair of the heart". Happiness comes from having a higher understanding of ourselves and a love for God and others deep within the human soul—*in the heart* where motives are shaped and commitments are generated and decisions are made.

In Shakespeare's play "Othello" the chief character describes his life of suffering and cries out, "My heart is turned to stone. I strike it and it hurts my hand." Many today have hearts of stone—inner beings hardened by circumstance and struggle and regret and cynicism so that there remains little vigor coursing through their veins.

I have seen how God can give men and women a new and stronger heart. Like the storm-battered but unbowed Jamaican gentleman sitting at my side in church, there are so many who have the Word planted deep within them and their lives bear continual fruit.

Long ago, in my home town of Indianapolis, I met a courageous African American mail carrier who volunteered as one of the early recipients of an artificial heart. This surgery was a wonderful breakthrough in medicine. The patient's life was lengthened for a time and, even though the quality of living was less than hoped for, the willing volunteer helped make medical history and could spend a few more weeks with his family.

We can anticipate one advancement after another in the field of cardiology. It is an exciting time of history when medical science is giving new life and hope again and again to those who, in years past, would not have lived beyond childhood.

Now I think again of my Jamaican friend and ask a deeper question: Will humankind allow God the Designer of Life and Jesus the Great Physician to put a "new heart" of love, mercy and goodness within us?

My soul prays the old gospel refrain embellished with a Caribbean lilt: *"Come into me heart, Lord Jesus."*

3

The Rock

One of the most venerated religious sites in the world is a large, unappealing slab of gray rock.

A "crown" atop Mount Moriah, this rocky protrusion has attracted millions of devout religious pilgrims across the centuries. It is the legendary stone on which the patriarch Abraham offered Isaac up in sacrifice. Jews know it as the traditional location of the temples of David and Solomon. It also is the place from which Muslims believe Mohammed began his ascent to heaven.

Mount Moriah in old Jerusalem—site of the Jews' Holy of Holies, the *Harem esh-Sharif* of sacred honor to Muslims, and the *Templum Domini* ("house of the Lord") to Crusaders—today features as its enclosure the great gilded mosque known as the Dome of the Rock. Nearby, on the same high ground called the "Temple Mount," is another smaller mosque.

There is a mystique about this hill that stands at the heart of the ancient walled city of Jerusalem. It is a prize that warrior king David captured from its earlier Canaanite occupants—and today one can see the excavated ruins of the ancient City of David just over the massive Herodian stones that form the foundation of the Temple Mount and frame the area below that is called the "wailing wall" or Western Wall.

Not everyone can come freely to Mount Moriah these days. I have always approached this segment of the tourist itinerary with both trepidation and expectation. Here one takes off shoes and truly stands on ground that is holy to three major religions of the world. One recognizes that the Muslim faith has control of the mount itself. Christians are allowed to visit briefly, under certain restrictions, but Jews are not generally permitted to set foot on the hill.

Here is a holy outcropping dedicated to God and yet is the scene of so much intrigue, death, divisiveness and destruction across hundreds of centuries! A beacon to the faithful but also a bloody stage where great tragedy has played out—from prehistory to the present day.

Not long ago, archeologists uncovered several flat stones leading from the foot of the Mount of Olives up to a closed entrance to the old city called the "Golden Gate". Jesus may have walked on these stones as he made his entry into the city on what Christians celebrate as "Palm Sunday".

As I stood on these slate-colored stones, looking above me toward the towering Temple Mount and resting for a moment in the shadow of massive walls built by successive generations of Jews, Christians and Muslim Turks, I sensed the power of the pervasive biblical image of *rock*. Everywhere there are stones, small and large—creating foundations, synagogues and shrines, houses, and holy sites. Palestine/Israel is a place of rugged stone homes and pathways and durable jigsaw-puzzle-like rock walls.

I have come to Mount Moriah on several occasions. Each time I have come away wondering how and when people of common ancestral faith will put aside their selfish concerns and together build a better order of peace and justice and liberty that will be a more fitting tribute to the One whom they unanimously hail as the True Rock on which all things stand firm.

◆   ◆   ◆

The churches I often visited in rural Indiana and Missouri seemed to have a special love for "rock music" in worship. It wasn't a particular beat but the reassuring *words* of certain hymns they liked to sing—hymns hailing the "Rock of Ages" or affirming "On Christ the Solid Rock I Stand" or entreating "Lead Me to the Rock".

This image has been appealing to me in trying to bring into sharper focus the often-elusive image of God in this present hour. Too many of life's structures seem to rest on what the old gospel song called "sinking sand". What was acceptable truth yesterday often is out of date or incomplete information today.

What can we build with some assurance that it will stand for a long period of time?

I have found special meaning in Jesus' parable of the houses built on sand and on rock. Obviously, it was the wiser man who built on a solid footing. His house was impervious to storms and floods.

Several years ago, the garage floor of our rather new home began to drop—an inch over a year or so, and then two and three more all in the space of a few weeks. We had a serious problem!

It seems that the builder not only placed our "attached" garage on a foundation separate from the main house itself, but he filled the space under the concrete garage floor with several inches of fine gravel and sand. Eventually, nature had its way and the whole slab began to sink.

Expensive piering had to be inserted deep into the underlying soil so that eventually we could create a solid base on which to pour a new and more durable concrete floor.

Too often in my lifetime I have watched as some trusted foundations in society began to crumble and sink, threatening to pull us all down into the underlying abyss. And there were those who did God's work by courageously digging down deeply and "setting the pierings" for such rock-like virtues as integrity, compassion, tolerance, decency, and selflessness.

At times Mount Moriah seems far away from my daily concerns. But I remember that this piece of blessed granite still is intact while the Herods and Caesars and all other bloody tyrants of history have become dust. Where shall I put my trust? An Oklahoma colleague used to ask me, "What do ya know fer sure?" Psalm 27 says it well: God *"will hide me in his shelter in the day of trouble; he will conceal me under the cover of his tent; he will set me high on a rock."*

4

Hope

"...suffering produces endurance, and endurance produces character, and character produces hope, and hope does not disappoint us, because God's love has been poured into our hearts...."

—(Romans 5:3b–5a)

Not many buildings were still whole in the little Mayan village we wanted to visit some forty miles outside Guatemala City.

The forlorn shell of a schoolhouse greeted us as we entered the rut-filled main street. We gripped our arm rests tightly as our Church World Service host dodged broken red roof tiles and other assorted rubble while cautiously piloting the well-worn minivan toward the main plaza.

"This is La Esperanza," the American mission representative said. "That word means 'hope', if you recall your Spanish. And these people sure needed a lot of it when the 'quake came."

We could imagine the scene of terror and devastation a few months earlier when the "big one" hit the heart of the scenic Central American nation, killing thousands as they slept and ripping apart an already fragile economy.

North American church members had been among the first to respond to the earthquake. Even before the United States and others had sent in the usual forms of material aid, Church World Service teams were on the scene providing shelter and food and counseling. Now a CWS representative wanted us to see some results of the churches' rapid response. Here in the central part of this incredibly beautiful country, where so many lost tools and the very raw *sources* of their livelihood, a fresh spirit of optimism was in the air. We could sense it in the smiles and warm handshakes—and in the sounds of hammers and tractors and playing children filling the air.

The people of La Esperanza made ceramic pottery for a living. Very little of it survived the earthquake, but—true to their village's name—the people still retained a lively spirit of hope within their hearts.

"Don't forget us," one artisan said. "Remember the hope that is here because you and others helped us in our need. You were doing God's work among us. Now we are rebuilding and at work at our kilns. Life is returning to normal."

On my office shelf I still keep an unpainted circular crèche made of clay—a gift from one Guatemalan potter. I also have a pair of doves produced for us as a special memento. Both are continual reminders that God puts an indestructible spirit of hope deep within the human heart. The birth of the Messiah came in the midst of an age of pain and despair for humankind. The doves rise above a broken earth and are lifted up by winds that will carry them to unprecedented new heights and vistas.

Earthquakes and assorted calamities may shatter the landscape and crush the fragile works of human hands, but the inner person may remain strong and whole and resilient—thanks to those who are God's emissaries of divine hope that "does not disappoint us".

On a number of occasions since that post-disaster visit to Guatemala, I have again taken the small ceramic objects into my hands, placed them in front of me, and thought of La Esperanza and its people.

For so many persons in our world—and for too many I meet in the course of my week-to-week activity—life seems to resemble more nearly the stark scene in the ancient Guatemalan town of Antigua—the early Spanish colonial capital. At Antigua a tourist feels compelled to pause in silent, somber reflection outside the ruins of a vast seventeenth-century monastery. Under the topsy-turvy pile of gigantic stone blocks, hundreds of young Spanish missionary priests lie entombed after an earthquake.

Hope is not an automatic gift after the world brings such tragedy and pain into our lives, as it so often does. Even the strongest need help in rebuilding a diminished sense of confidence and purpose. I have continued to welcome all those who, deliberately or perhaps unwittingly, assist me in regaining hope by their supportive words and compassionate gestures that ease the hurt. And then I find myself making a vow to be a more consistent bearer of hope to others, using all of the various means God gives me.

◆   ◆   ◆

One of my high, exhilarating moments as an interim college chaplain came during the visit to the campus of Terry Waite, the Anglican layman who was held captive and in isolation for 1,763 days by Middle Eastern terrorists. Waite, a gentle man of peace, suffered more than any of us could even imagine, but he was an ambassador of hope as he spoke to students at Culver-Stockton College in Canton, Missouri.

Relating his frustrating career as a would-be peacemaker and rescuer and his sudden capture and long imprisonment, Waite did not display the bitterness many of us would rightly feel. He kept his focus on his original mission of bringing divided, warring factions closer together, freeing other captives, and brokering a durable peace.

Waite told, of course, of his deep confidence that God had never abandoned him. A divine presence brightening the darkness was vivid and comforting. But he also told of one day receiving a solitary postcard delivered by a captor. The card showed a picture of writer-dissident-theologian John Bunyan sitting in jail. The sender, from distant England, wrote: "We shall not forget, we shall continue to pray for you and work for all who are detained around the world."

Terry Waite was sustained in hope by some distant, nameless comrade he would never meet.

Each day I discover emissaries of hope at work on my behalf. They will not let me get down on myself or on the world God has formed and loves eternally. I pray I will have the insight and courage to build a community of *La Esperanza* right where I live and labor.

5

Genuine

"Religion that is pure and undefiled before God, the Father, is this: to care for orphans and widows in their distress, and to keep oneself unstained by the world."

—(James 1:27)

I still miss the voice of my college roommate, Ned, who would call me periodically from Pittsburgh—where he served as a professor on a university faculty—and begin needling me with some salutation such as this:

"Well, old Roomie, I was reading in the news about Evangelist 'So-and-So' this week and how he's in trouble again with the IRS, and I thought about you. What do you have to say?"

Ned wanted to get in his two cents about all the golden-tongued, media-savvy, money-hungry religious personalities who continue to enlarge their loyal and gullible followings—until they are brought low by greed, silliness or sexual misdeeds.

My old friend wasn't hostile to all expressions of religious faith. Although he didn't please his more traditional church-going parents by his absence from the pews most weekends, he was a solid thinker with as astronomical IQ who pondered the Big Questions in late-night gab sessions at our fraternity house. He even appreciated the colorful (and brief) sermons by the popular minister of the Methodist church near campus.

Ned's ire was directed toward those who weren't honest or honorable in their practice of faith. He had a nose that detected the fakers, the power lovers, the social climbers, and those he once called the "syrupy simpletons".

I didn't have any real answers for Ned except to assure him that I knew many clergy who reflected just the opposite of his stereotyped evangelist-healer-huckster picture.

As a teenager, a friend and I went one summer Sunday afternoon to a vacant lot near my home. A traveling faith healer had set up shop in a sweltering big tent there. It was my first up-close encounter with those who "peddled" religion as a product one could purchase with dollars or with a raised-arm, tearful walk down the sawdust trail.

Fortunately, I was exposed to a more *healthy* side of religion through participation in a warm mainstream congregation where the leadership was intellectually honest, teachers were dedicated to *living* the Scriptures, and the clergy seemed to be self-sacrificial in their personal behavior.

◆   ◆   ◆

So much religious news these days concerns the sad antics of pious empire-builders, glib spiritual showmen (and women), and televised plati-tude-preachers, prophets and gurus who are saying the same old stuff for the thousandth time but convincing their audiences that they have just invented the wheel!

My quarrel with all religious hucksters is not as fierce as it once was because I have watched more and more of the notorious ones self-destruct. My frustration continues, though, because so many potential believers today are like my old college friend Ned. They echo Gandhi's reputed response to Methodist missionary E. Stanley Jones, who had asked him why he never became a Christian, seeing that he lived by so many of the Christian virtues. "I would be a Christian," Gandhi is reported to have said, "were it not for the fact that I have met so many *Christians*."

I have found it hard to square my understanding of Jesus' message of self-forgetting service with the crass commercialism and hype present on today's wider religious stage.

It helps me, though, to remember that the problem did not start with Father Charles Coughlin or evangelists Aimee Semple McPherson and Buford Cadle when they and scores of other charismatic religious personalities discovered the power of the radio pulpit in the depth of the Great Depression.

The prophets of ancient Israel and Judah had to deal with retaliatory "competitors" who sold their voices and their influence—and their souls—to the highest bidders. The apostles won no friends when they denounced those silversmiths and wood carvers who made and sold pagan idols for a living.

My wife and I once attended a worship service in a Pentecostal church when the infamous Jim Jones still lived in Indianapolis and was not yet arranging to take his People's Temple contingent to San Francisco. Jones was a remarkably personable young man. One could have some sympathy for him at first. He was a fundamentalist with a deep social consciousness, and some in the mainline churches were enamored by this unusual blend. He had been hounded for his interracial work in a city where the divide between black and white was a chasm.

Jones, no doubt, was a sick man both physically and mentally. Sadly, he took dozens of gullible followers (including some of our daughter's high school classmates) to their death at Jonestown.

I wish I could pick up my phone and talk with my old friend Ned again. There are some further apologies I would make. The worldwide depth of religious arrogance, greed, foolishness and pretense may be higher today than ever before. We still have not learned that true biblical faith calls for humility, sacrifice, clear thinking and transparency before the God who knows us well and judges us for our thoughts as well as our deeds.

All I can do now is remember and in my prayers say, "Thanks, Roomie! May I always try to heed the Apostle Paul's stern advice to the Roman church: "Let love be genuine...."

6

Faithful

"The faithful will abound with blessings...."

—(Proverbs 28:20a)

We first realized that our friend Margaretlou ("Mickie") had a problem when we saw her stumble a few times as we met for dinner. We looked forward to our brief visits with Mickie and her husband, Norb, while on vacation near their home on the Florida Gulf Coast.

Mickie and my wife knew each other from childhood days and had kept in touch over the years. We attended the couple's big wedding in Cincinnati and celebrated with them as children came along and both of our families grew.

Now, all of us approaching middle age and its risks, we were concerned because the woman we knew as active and vibrant was slurring some words and tottering off-balance as she arose from her chair. Very soon we had our shocking introduction to Huntington's, a neurological disorder akin to ALS ("Lou Gehrig's Disease") and its debilitating medical cousins.

We saw Mickie and Norb many times in the succeeding years, and at each visit we would observe a steady decline in our friend's condition. She would enter the hospital briefly from time to time, but Norb insisted that she stay in their home so he could take care of her personally.

In the wedding vows exchanged by most couples there is some version of the traditional line: *"...for better or for worse, in sickness and in health."* Norb made such a promise to Mickie half a century earlier and did not forget! He became his Sweetheart's hands and voice and nutritionist and chauffeur—hour after hour, around the clock. In between gently caring

16

for her, Norb managed to find a few hours to help at his nearby Catholic parish and to assist a food pantry.

After Mickie's quiet passing, following years of silent suffering, Norb did not want to be seen as a heroic figure. "She was my Sweetie," he said. "When I stood before the altar and made a promise to her before God, I intended to keep it."

◆　　◆　　◆

The bold assurance of Scripture that God is faithful is easier now for me to grasp and savor—thanks to Norb and to dozens of other men and women who have shown me what that word means in the practical matters of daily living.

Through God's gift of friendship, I was able to know a man who cared about his spouse genuinely, endlessly, tenderly—and at times, to those who watched this continuing love affair, *amazingly!*

As I study and ponder the story of faith in the Scriptures I see this same wonder expressed by people as they finally begin to comprehend the faithfulness of God. I continue to be a glad recipient myself of that unwavering divine compassion and mercy.

An aging and ailing Jack Buck, the premier sports broadcaster for the St. Louis "Cardinal Nation," told a reporter that he had one question to ask God when (and if) he entered the gates of heaven. He wanted to ask his Creator, "Lord, why have you been so good to me?"

At times I have pondered a similar question as I observed the ways in which a faithful God called out to me, challenged me, and upheld and guided me with a loving commitment deeper even than that which I witnessed in my dear friend Norb.

Why does God remain so steadfast, even when we fail many times to keep our end of the covenant? Why do we get second and third—and more—chances to do better? The Apostle Paul surely kept pondering this question which he first asked when blindsided by the Lord on the road to Damascus. He returns to it again and again in his writings, as we see in *2*

Timothy 2:13 when he quotes a rabbinical saying, "If we are faithful, he remains faithful—for he cannot deny himself."

My friend Norb was steadfast because God had so taken charge of his life and thought that this good man could not possibly "deny himself". Caring for his ill wife was a characteristic formed in the very depth of his being.

My years have been enriched by so many who merit the words of praise Jesus heaped upon the worthy steward in the parable of the talents: "Well done, good and *faithful* servant….Enter into the joy of your Lord."

In the life of all the churches I have known there have been special men and women sometimes mildly scorned or ridiculed as "the faithful few". They are the ones who attend most every function, who volunteer first when asked, who turn on lights and shut them out.

I admire those "faithful few" because they help me have a clearer picture of God.

Consider a farmer named Paul—obscurely positioned in a small rural community in Indiana and elder in a congregation whose student preachers came and went on a regular basis over the years.

Paul was a quiet fellow. Faith for him was basic, unsophisticated, a clear matter of right versus wrong and "Thus saith the Lord". He did not budge mountains of sin as a Christian but he did stand at the door of the one-room white framed country chapel and tell me, "Son, don't worry. If no one else is here on Sunday, you can count on me. I'll open up, wipe off the pews, fix communion, and lock up afterwards. You just get here yourself. I'll take care of the Lord's House."

"Well done, good and faithful servant!"

Well done, servant Norb. You have been steadfast in caring for the one you took as your own flesh and promised to love "'til death us do part."

Well done, servant Paul. You helped a young preacher understand that when he expounded on the "great mercy of God" and urged folks in the pews to be more persistent, there was a living witness there every week on the front pew—or standing outside the church door with his key ready to lock up when the flock headed home!

7

Father

"As a father has compassion for his children, so the Lord has compassion for those who fear him."

—(Psalms 103:13)

It wasn't surprising that most of my childhood friends either had an absentee father or none at all. It was wartime, and many men in the 35–50 age bracket were in military service. A few dads were "off somewhere", as my folks put it, perhaps still trying to piece their lives together or make some war-time dollars after suffering through the Great Depression.

Church was one place where some of us could find a substitute father. A "real" one couldn't be replaced fully by any of the paunchy middle-aged males in starched white shirts who ushered or served communion on Sundays, but we fondly looked to most of them for their weekly wisdom, periodic pats on the back, and fairly regular lectures on discipline.

We heard and talked a great deal in Sunday School and worship about God as "Father". By standards many of us take for granted today, our religious language then was decidedly sexist, but we weren't troubled by it. We kids knew in our hearts what the Bible meant in using that decidedly "male" description of the Almighty. No offense to mothers was intended. We already saw and heard from them ninety percent of the time, and we understood even before the advent of a women's movement that God is not a bearded Nordic grandfather figure sitting in his throne on some heavenly cloud.

We who were children hungering for more male "presence" in our lives were drawn to those strong and good men we met in church—and when we heard continual references by ministers and Sunday School teachers to our "Father God" we made pleasant connections in our minds and hearts that stayed with us the rest of our lives.

Jesus said that a "good father" will not "give his child a stone when he asks for bread." We knew of some real-life, present-day dads whose legacy was harsh and unwholesome and stony-hearted. But we saw the *other* kind—the one described in that Aramaic word *Abba* that Jesus used in speaking of God—a word akin to our own tender "Daddy".

So much of what we discovered in those formative years about the nature of God didn't come from pulpit or teacher's lecture or faded Ten Commandments filmstrip projected on a wall. The real message about God came from those kind, patient, honorable men around us—those substitute dads—who were trying to live out what they believed.

◆   ◆   ◆

Mr. B was far from being a dynamic, animated speaker and teacher. He admitted that his raspy voice and self-effacing persona had been a strong factor in his decision not to pursue ministry as his grandfather and father had done.

Always in the headlines as chief executive of our city's powerful Chamber of Commerce, Mr. B was better known to our church's young people as the quiet guy who sat and talked with us each Sunday about issues of life and faith.

He was the father of two boys who were part of our youth group—one son a handsome, athletic, head-of-his class type of fellow; the other, a severely disabled boy whose cerebral palsy left him unable to walk or to speak effectively.

What impressed us most was not the wisdom that Mr. B shared with us each week—or the way he managed to quietly provoke discussion. We saw him physically carry his disabled son up three flights of stairs on Sunday morning so the boy could be a part of our class. Every step was labored. We seemed to be watching a movie in slow-motion. The slick marble was a challenging hazard and the son increased in dead weight year after year.

But the scenario continued—right up to the time we all left high school and headed off to college or similar ventures.

What did we learn in church and Sunday school as we studied about God as "our Father" and prayed the Lord's Prayer, addressing our petitions to "Our Father who art in heaven"? We read all the usual commentary and talked about words such as *love, patience, discipline*, and *forgiveness* that should characterize a good parent's relationship with a child. But it was that little drama taking place before and after class every Sunday that brought home to us the deepest and highest meaning of fatherhood.

Mr. B was a man of few and sometimes whispery words, but in everything he *did* he demonstrated with power the faith that was in his heart.

I still cling to the ancient picture of God as *Father*—not as the only view of the Creator that is adequate but surely as one word that for me brings back an indelible image from my youth. I still see Mr. B gently but firmly holding on to his son Billy—not letting him fall, speaking words of encouragement in his ear each tough step upward toward the goal. I see the smile on both of their faces when they reach the third-floor landing—and there is joy all around as others surround and embrace them.

Mr. B was not the only good dad I met as I was growing toward maturity. Dozens and dozens of them crossed my path along the way. Each had a different temperament, often a peculiarity or two, certainly some weakness that proved he was human. We never believed we were surrounded by perfect men. But we saw that these mentors of ours were humble and never pretended to be more than they were. We knew they cared for more than themselves, that they wanted those kids who became their proxy "family" to have a better life than they had known—one free of hatred, prejudice, poverty and ignorance.

I pray: "May the God and Father of our Lord Jesus Christ bless *all* 'fathers' of the world. May dads, granddads, uncles and all male friends of youth know how important they are and what a rich legacy they can leave—even if they don't realize it. May the spirit of Mr. B live in us all!"

8

Mother

"The eye that...scorns to obey a mother will be pecked out by the ravens of the valley and eaten by the vultures."

—*(Proverbs 30:17)*

The firm words of a young woman behind me at the checkout counter could be heard all over the supermarket:

"Be still! Listen to your momma!"

Right away, the preschooler tugging at her mother's jacket quit her nonstop fidgeting and insistent begging, making the afternoon more pleasant for several of us in the vicinity.

If there is any phrase that captures the global saga of womanhood in recent times, it might be found in these four little words of a weary, impatient parent required to handle dollars-and-cents trivia while being asked to fulfill the huge role of nurturer: *"Listen to your momma!"*

Sometimes moms get tired of the thousand demands made upon them and decide to deal only with larger issues. Often they grow weary of being forced to yield control of their thoughts and actions—and bodies. And that's when anyone around finds out that it's much better not to mess with momma. Even Scripture warns about the danger of disobeying a mother. The result would be like getting your eyes pecked out by the ravens, *Proverbs* says. Tough punishment!

I learned the power of riled-up women (and the men they won over to their side) when the world's largest maker of infant formula began aggressively marketing its product in the Third World without asking where mothers in an African village might readily find safe water to mix with the milk powder.

As an editor with so many issues to look at, I was not particularly knowledgeable—or excited—about this one. But international church bodies took up this cause, prodded by mission-related doctors and nurses who had seen first-hand how pre-packaged infant formula can fail to meet the needs in remote places of the world and even can be deadly. I learned a lot about breast feeding that was never taught in seminary or that the obstetrician who delivered our three children never liked to talk about. (I remember that he always had free samples of patented formula to hand out with every office visit!)

The worldwide Nestle Corporation, which later became a stronger advocate of "natural" feeding, more sterile formula preparation, and responsible advertising, learned that one does not dare provoke the moms of the world or those who care about their welfare. The united voice of women and their friends proved to be loud and persuasive! Women have enormous buying power. And they have influence over presidents, prime ministers and assorted princes!

To me, moving personally from detached ignorance to mild inquisitiveness and then to thorough commitment, this so-called "formula campaign" was one of the finest hours for the Christian community around the globe. People who differed widely in matters of theology and politics came together in response to an issue that affected the welfare of those who are the bearers of life and the nurturers of humankind.

◆   ◆   ◆

I have been grateful for the insistent voice of concerned motherhood.

One rainy May morning a missionary in Buenos Aires invited me to join him on a downtown street in the Argentine capital. He said he wanted me to watch the "march of the mothers".

I don't know what I expected, but the scene I witnessed will always stay with me. By the hundreds and hundreds they came, silently, somberly—these "Madres de la Plaza de Mayo". Many bore poster-size photos of sons and husbands who were officially labeled "missing" but were known to be victims of the government's assassination squads.

The free world largely distanced itself from the Perón regime and all the oppression that was transpiring on its watch. There were too many other battles to fight. But the mothers of those who had disappeared issued a silent but penetrating and persistent cry: "Hear us! You have taken our men; you have destroyed our families. You must give an account!"

And they won their fight.

Mothers all across the world possess an amazing force. Sometimes their struggle for respect and justice has taken a long, long time but today in some lands and cultures is *nearly* won. In some places the fight is just beginning. But those who value the message of the Bible know that this is a work in which God has a strong hand.

At the Cross Jesus pointed to Mary and told some of the disciples, "Here is your mother".

I think of this message of breadth and inclusiveness whenever I celebrate the May holiday we call Mothers Day (which in many churches is a high holy day surpassing even Easter!).

In visiting central Africa, I was impressed with the way that so many people in villages and in big cities would often refer to more mature women as *"Mama"*. It does not matter if a woman is young or older, or has borne children, or if she is related to the one offering this expression of recognition. In the understanding of many across central Africa, a person has *many* mothers. *All women* share in common the important role of community nurture and education. *All* deserve to be respected, heard and followed.

As I have tried to hear a "word from the Lord" across the years, answers at times have not been all that loud or clear. But I've had little doubt when God has spoken through the words and deeds of those who are the biological or spiritual mothers of the earth. The message still resounds: "Pay attention to mommas everywhere. Listen and learn! There's big trouble ahead whenever you don't—and many blessings when you *do*!"

9

Age

"…I will pour out my spirit on all flesh; your sons and your daughters shall prophesy, your old men shall dream dreams, and your young men shall see visions."

—(Joel 2:28)

The lounge area of the rambling county-seat nursing home was brighter than usual. Gigantic, colorful ribbons were attached to the utilitarian steel chairs, and a big five-layer decorated cake was placed in the middle of the tables that had been pulled together into a great square.

I was late in arriving for the special birthday party that Mabel's children had arranged to celebrate her ninetieth year. Some polite words had already been spoken when I entered the room and—as a good pastor is generally allowed to do—put my hand on her shoulder, gave her a gentle hug, and said, "Mabel, this is a great day for you. Congratulations and God bless you!"

Without looking up, Mabel launched into a speech prefaced with some of the strongest "cuss words" I could recall. Her conclusion, punctuated again by a heavy dose of sailor's vocabulary, was that it is not very much fun to get old!

We all laughed politely. Her embarrassed son, a well-known local political leader, apologized.

"Mom always did have a salty tongue," he observed.

Eager to get finished with the now-tense party, we all sang "Happy birthday!", quickly cut the cake into several pieces, and went our way after a few minutes of small talk, still trying to see the humorous side of what had just happened.

Anyone living long enough knows the painful truth of a popular bumper sticker slogan: "Aging Isn't for Cowards". But there's not much we can do, in this era of medical marvels and legal restraints, to slow or to halt the process. It's best just to go along for the ride and make the most of it no matter how creaky and crabby we get.

We do have a right to "cuss out life" at times—as the poet Dylan Thomas implied—refraining from "going gently into that good night," and determined to "rage, rage, against the dying of the light."

My own experience is that aging really isn't such a fearsome enemy. For many, "senior status" can be the time of their greatest contentment, their most enjoyable and straightforward relationships, a strong sense of satisfaction, the wisest decision-making, and the period of deepest spiritual sensitivity. True, it takes longer to get out of bed and there are far too many bottles of pills on the bathroom shelf—and we may not be able to stay up to watch all the late shows on television the way we once did. But aging offers so many unique rewards.

◆   ◆   ◆

Well past her one hundredth birthday, my high school journalism teacher—Jean—was still looking forward to visits from her former pupils (one a U.S. Senator and another a prize-winning author) and always eager to learn about each member of every family connected with her very large circle of friendship. Jean had sturdy genes, of course, but it was her inquisitiveness and her love for others that gave zest to her mind when her body may have been ready to give up.

Only a short time ago, it was headline news when someone celebrated a centennial milestone. Now such birthday anniversaries are becoming commonplace. There are a dozen on our family's Christmas mailing list who are 85 and above, and I anticipate being of sound mind, if not *body*, and still corresponding with them when they pass the Big 100 mark.

The American challenge now, I conclude, is not to prolong life. This is happening as a matter of course. The bigger task for all of us is to make sure that the *quality* of life continues as the months and years are extended.

That may mean encouraging older persons to be as active and involved in society as they desire and as they are able. It also may mean doing more to support those who are finding their golden years to be tarnished by infirmity, poverty and loneliness.

A retiree friend, Glenn, has made his own senior years count by volunteering in a hospice program. He is energized by expressing his religious faith in visits with those who are terminally ill.

Another friend, when a centenarian, was still reading to toddlers at a day-care center for children with special needs.

I have met an 80-year-old surgeon who still offers his advice, if not his arthritic hands, to the staffs operating free clinics in poor areas of his own town and in villages of Africa and Latin America.

Food pantries in my city would close up tomorrow without the volunteer labor of men and women well into their seventies and eighties.

It is good to see so many active seniors reaching out to share their gifts—generally receiving a "paycheck" that is no more than a 50-cent certificate or a yearly appreciation luncheon.

But I will never forget Billy Bob, the old vagrant with the Tennessee twang who came twice a year to our church with the same sad old story. Billy Bob never remembered he had been at our doorstep before. He told the same tale of woe and pulled from his tattered billfold the same crumpled stack of preacher calling cards that he said would vouch for his honesty. His mind was frazzled from years of sleeping under bridges and drinking cheap booze. He came for so many years—and I missed him when he no longer knocked at our church office door.

For some of us, the years are challenging but also kind, gentle and rewarding. For others, like fragile little Billy Bob—or Mabel—aging is a bitter passage from death to death. Where I can help those who walk with me down the "home stretch" but can't see how to reach the goal, I promise to reach out and extend my hand!

10

Peace

"...a time to love and a time to hate; a time for war, and a time for peace."

—(Ecclesiastes 3:8b)

The 278-foot statue near the Volga River was visible from our Aeroflot plane well before we touched down at Volgograd.

We heard about the massive sword-wielding *Rodina Mat' Zovyot* ("Mother Motherland Is Calling") long before we reached the Ukraine to make a fraternal church visit in the former Stalingrad. Previous guests of the Russian Orthodox Churches had told us that the huge 7,900-ton monument, erected in 1967, might well qualify as a modern wonder of the world.

We agreed with earlier visitors! "Mother Motherland"—one of several enormous war monuments erected across the former Soviet Union—draws a heavy emotional response from even the casual observer. It is clear that something happened near this site that touched the hearts of ordinary men and women in a deep and lasting way.

Stalingrad. To those in any way familiar with the Eastern front in World War II, this name still evokes the image of stubborn, head-to-head, to-the-death military conflict. It is a name that symbolizes heroism. It asks the question: *"What if....?"* Could this pleasant, bustling industrial town, with its riverside museum-park featuring bombed-out buildings and a few rusting tanks, be the place where the war against fascism at last took a turn in favor of "our" side?

The great statue standing guard over old Stalingrad is designed to be a forceful reminder to complacent, self-absorbed, present-day citizens of the

28

"motherland" who—as it is with all of us—tend to forget the price paid for freedom and opportunity.

I have visited war monuments and military cemeteries in scores of lands. The battles may have been quite different in style and in purpose. But they never fail to leave some impression on one's mind and soul.

Standing at the ruins of Megiddo in Israel, I looked out across the beautiful green valleys below and remembered the reason that ancient tradition and contemporary "Last Days" apocalyptic writings argue that the final battle—*Armageddon*—will be fought in this tranquil spot. From the earliest centuries, the area near Megiddo was the place where opposing armies marched West to East and North to South and fought and killed thousands without mercy.

Far more statues and monuments and museums are dedicated to *death* than to life! This is a fact of human history. And for me, if there is any value in building and maintaining so many of these elaborate and expensive memorials, it is in order to help us recall the brutality of warfare. The marble pillars, soothing background music (at Volgograd it is Liszt's "Liebenstraum") and lovely flowered tributes touch our deepest senses, as they should. But all of it is wasted unless the visitor comes away with a deepened appreciation of the human cost of war and the absolute necessity of working to prevent future carnage.

Two war memorials have been especially impressive for me.

Standing in the small but majestic military cemetery at Normandy, one can look down toward the sea and, if sturdy and brave enough, walk down closer to get a better look at Omaha Beach and the other Allied landing areas where so many troops met their death on D-Day.

A visitor finds it hard to stop the flow of tears. But this is part of what a military cemetery is supposed to do. So it is with the *Arizona* monument at Pearl Harbor. As one stands over a turret of that sunken battleship and remembers that it is, in reality, a tomb for hundreds, there is an overpowering sense of awe and sadness.

Jews and Christians are people whose faith calls them to remember. But always the conclusion is *"remember…so that life may be different for future generations."*

I have conducted many interment services at Jefferson Barracks National Cemetery in St. Louis. Sometimes, when military "honors" are warranted, the music of "Taps" will be played using a recording and a scratchy portable sound system. Thanks to volunteers—many of them advanced in years—more and more final rites make use of live trumpeters. I like to watch the honor guard closely, especially when it is made up of senior veterans who see these services as a mission. Many men and women are a bit too weighty for their old uniforms. Some are slow and a little rusty in presenting arms. One or two get so emotionally absorbed in their task that they hardly make it through to the end.

These veterans always inspire me. I want to salute them. No matter how or when they served their nation, they have some dimension of the heroic in their blood.

In some of his writings from a Pacific island during the waning days of World War II, correspondent Ernie Pyle reflected a growing anger over the senseless brutality of modern warfare but a deep appreciation for those who fought bravely when they had to answer their nation's call. "They were good men and women, all of them," Pyle observed.

I had that same feeling as I stood at Normandy and as I climbed to Megiddo. It came upon me while walking over the Civil War battlefield of Antietam…as I saw where William the Conqueror's forces stood strong at Hastings…and as I visited the site at which Napoleon truly "met his Waterloo".

Remembrance of wars past is important. Such continual introspection—with the trouble and tears that accompany it—honors those who have played an important role in preserving for us many of the good things we take for granted.

We have had what *Ecclesiates* speaks of as "a time to hate…a time for war." Now can battered humankind, recalling history, spend more effort to preserve, honor and extend "a time for *peace*"?

11

Teacher

"As he went ashore, he saw a great crowd; and he had compassion for them, because they were like sheep without a shepherd; and he began to teach them many things."

—(Mark 6:34)

The hazards of being a public school teacher were obvious to anyone required to sit for a few moments in the office of Principal Olive K. Funk, who believed in running "her" School No. 45 by a military-school code.

From any one of the four polished oak chairs in her tiny office, a "guest" could see the stained-glass window behind her desk and note the very obvious BB hole that served as an unintended punctuation mark for the slogan imprinted thereon: "Knowledge Is Power".

The famous Francis Bacon statement represented an *ideal* that motivates most educators I have known: *to offer to learners a life of power by helping them expand their knowledge.* The air-gun "wound" represented the *reality* of that task: to teach kids something of deeper value while the thundering message of the world is that might and money always trump fact and reason!

But Miss F. kept *trying*, as did every other teacher I knew in that school. And even though her mission must at times have seemed impossible, she lived long enough to see many of her most aggravating pupils turn into fairly decent young men and women.

If a child is fortunate, he or she will have a few dozen memorable teachers—from kindergarten on through the upper levels of learning. They will on occasion show some gaps in actual "book facts", given the rapid expansion of human knowledge. They will have personality quirks to irritate us

31

and may pamper a few overly zealous students who court special favor. Teachers are, after all, human. But each one makes some long-term impact on our mind and character.

I still recall my kindergarten teacher, Mrs. V, who saw that I was a "momma's boy" needing some extra attention at first—before the apron strings from home could even be loosened just a bit…. and I remember Mr. M, who knew I would in later life need at least *some* acquaintance with hammer and saw even if I would never build anything other than an ugly classroom project that fell apart in two days….and there was Mrs. B of the seventh grade, who didn't laugh when I told her I was writing a great novel but said, "I'll be glad to make little corrections when you're finished."

Every teacher I encountered added one or more vital, positive ingredients to the mix. The growing and changing and maturing process started on my first day of school and continued on through four years of seminary.

In reflection today, I can see a providential hand at work in this learning process. I was fortunate to have those instructors and administrators who somehow realized—as one saying puts it—that "teachers affect eternity…one never knows where their influence will end".

• John S. was the chair of our university's journalism department. A crusty ex-newspaperman, he was rough on all of us when we were lax in our spelling and grammar or were sloppy note-takers. If you got any commendation from Mr. S (or "St. John", as we called him because he loved to sign off on his critiques as "stj"), it was a slight nod and a half-smile. His sense of humor was constrained but irreverently hilarious. He once pointed to some 4-inch block letters of headline type and noted that he was "saving these for the Second Coming".

Some faculty members were open about their religious commitments (and also their skepticism), but John never talked about matters of faith—until that day I asked him to write a letter to my seminary noting that I was planning to prepare for "full-time Christian service".

With the same scowl he used when telling me my news story was poorly organized, he took off his wire-rimmed glasses, looked me in the eye and asked, "Jim, what the h—is 'full-time Christian service'? *I'm* a Christian. I go to church and try to follow the Bible every day in my life. *Isn't that what you would call a full-time Christian?*"

"St. John" had me cornered, as always, with his dry wit posing the *real* question that needed to be asked about my future plans. He gave me my first "sermon" on the *nature of the laity*—one that I have since repeated in dozens of settings. Aren't *all* who follow Jesus supposed to be engaged in "full-time Christian service"?

I have remembered that exchange through the years. From this master newspaperman, teacher and friend I learned to look beyond the surface of issues, to seek truth even when it's carefully hidden, and never to be content with rhetoric, propaganda and hastily drawn conclusions.

● Miss D. *had* to accompany her graduation well wishes with a bit of Latin. That was her field. She started teaching Virgil and Cicero, some suggested, when these authors were still alive!

A prim, plain-dressing, single older woman teaching an obscure "dead" language, she was the stereotype one often sees in satirical literature and in comic books.

Her beautifully handwritten note—which I still have and sometimes revisit—contains two words, *Carpe Diem*, followed by "Warm wishes to you, always." She echoed Horace, her favorite poet, in hoping that I might "seize the day"—make good use of time—make every moment count.

Miss D. left no family. She never accumulated a substantial bank account. I doubt that she ever got to visit the homeland of Cicero, Horace and their kin. As far as I know, she didn't receive any high honors. But her adoring pupils never forgot her. When decision-time came and one had to choose between lethargy and action, between acquiescence to evil and struggle on behalf of what is right and good, those funny Latin words kept coming back: *Carpe diem*!

12

Laughter

"Then Abraham fell on his face and laughed...."

—(Genesis 17:17a)

Dave was a first-year seminarian who had lived enough years and had gained sufficient experience to be deemed worthy of a part-time student pastorate along the Missouri River near St. Louis.

He was an outgoing fellow with an exceptional wit. Friends at the seminary and those who knew him as a neighbor all appreciated his ever-smiling demeanor and re-told many of his jokes.

One day after worship, an older lay leader of the congregation informed Dave that he should no longer tell funny stories from the pulpit. It was out of place, the man contended—something "not proper" in the house of God. After all, the sturdy, hard-working, God-fearing German settlers who established that congregation a century earlier would not approve.

Colleagues had little help to offer Dave, except to note that his parish apparently was cursed with a number of misguided sourpusses. Most congregations—including the one I was serving at the time—are blessed with happy folk who welcome a lighter touch from the pulpit instead of constant grim, thunder-and-lightning "Thus saith the Lord!" pronouncements.

I hope Dave has remained in the ministry because Christians are supposed to be happy. The deeper word for it is "joy"—an ever-present confidence that existence has purpose and that our own days have value. When we have this inner gladness we *have* to laugh at ourselves and at life!

◆   ◆   ◆

Larry, a deacon in my suburban congregation, liked to torment me. He thought that his 38-year-old pastor was becoming a suburban stuffed shirt. So just before the start of worship, he would often sneak up and whisper one of the worst of many jokes and anecdotes he had heard during the previous week. Just when I caught the punch line, the organist would start the processional hymn and Larry would send me off down the aisle while he looked on with a satisfied grin on his face.

I am thankful to Larry, because he helped me realize that laughter in the house of the Lord is quite proper.

◆   ◆   ◆

Joe was a prominent pastor in my state and a popular luncheon-circuit speaker. There were months when he probably got checks for telling hilarious stories that were larger than those he received for sermonizing.

Joe was worth whatever he was paid for his presentation entitled "The Therapy of Laughter". He kept some of the best jokes as a staple in his speeches, but he always added new material gathered from the day's headlines.

I heard Joe a dozen times but never failed to join in the hearty guffaws right from the start when he repeated the old line we had heard so many times before—that he had proudly graduated from college as his brother did; but in the brother's case it was *magna cum laude* while in *his* situation, friends and family would say, "Laudy, how come?"

Joe helped me appreciate the value of humor in illustrating a theological point, in breaking through walls to make contact with "unreachable" people, and in simply expressing joy at being alive and having a reason to continue the journey.

◆   ◆   ◆

One of the greatest religious commentator-humorists of our time was Halford Luccock, venerable seminary professor at Yale and long-time columnist (*"Simeon Stylites"*) for the *Christian Century*. Others have tried to duplicate his style but have never quite measured up. He had a special gift for probing the foibles and pretenses of the day with tongue in cheek.

As both a pastor and a denominational staffer, I could appreciate Luccock's tale of the little town in the Midwest that was flooded following a lengthy rain. Church leaders were befuddled and fearful. The mail carrier could not get through on the rain-covered roads to bring to the church next week's "official pronouncements from headquarters." So after much agitated prayer, the church leaders sadly agreed that there was nothing else they could do the following Sunday "except to worship God".

My favorite Luccock story was one told to illustrate a speech presented for a city-wide ecumenical rally. His joke seemed out of place at the time—and somewhat risqué for that period—but it offered amazing insight into one of the major sources of conflict between different faith traditions.

Luccock told the story of the woman who went to a sewing goods store and asked for 50 yards of material with which to make her bridal nightgown. The clerk was surprised and said, "Ma'am, you don't need that much, do you?"

"Yes," the bride-to-be replied, "my husband and I are both Unitarians and we believe it is more important to *seek* than to *find*."

I got the point then—and have remembered it. There is, as I have learned, a big difference in the way good Christians look at the "rules" of faith—as being cast firmly and clearly in stone, or as matters for continual "seeking" and "finding".

Earlier in my life, I probably accepted a puritanical view that it isn't right or polite to jest a lot—especially before God. But as the years have come and gone, I've learned that it's the *only* way one can survive. It *is* a serious and sometimes brutally grim world, to be sure—and God keeps putting a melody of joy, love and hope in the human heart. Whatever God gives us is good and has to be shared!

Keep laughing!

13

Language

"Amazed and astonished, they asked, 'Are not all these who are speaking Galileans? And how is it that we hear, each of us, in our own language?'"

—(Acts 2:7–8)

One small letter can make a huge difference, as a distinguished mission representative found when he assisted in the ordination of a woman pastor in Argentina.

The incident has now become a humorous legend, but at the time it was an embarrassing moment and probably confirmed the picture some Latin Americans have of North Americans as poor linguists who are insensitive to cultural differences. Fortunately, the Argentines chuckled to themselves—and the missionary, so the story goes, never even realized what he had said!

In Spanish there is a good verb for "ordain"—*ordinar*. But there is also a slightly different version, using the Spanish "*ñ*" (*ordiñar*), which means to "milk a cow".

The latter verb is the one the visitor used, again and again, as he praised the honoree.

Language is one mark of division, but it also can have the *opposite* effect. Words can draw people together when we realize that all the sentences we speak and put into writing are but varied expressions of the ideas and dreams we share as humankind. When I have probed and pushed beyond strange nouns and verbs and idioms, I often have found amazing unanimity.

◆   ◆   ◆

Trying to save a few dollars, I arranged with the travel agency to have a local, independent coach driver serve our tour group as we traveled to Spain and Portugal. I asked that the driver be able to double as both a chauffeur and a verbal guide.

When Juan, our driver, met us at the airport in Lisbon he greeted us in *Spanish*. When I asked him a question, he responded again in *Spanish*.

There was no time to ask myself why I hadn't brushed up on my rusty college Español before departure or why in the world I hadn't double-checked with the travel agency to make sure we were to be given a *bilingual* driver!

We smiled, extended our hands and I said, "*Mucho gusto, Juan*....and, by the way, do you understand *any Ingles?*"

What followed were ten delightful days. I would sit in the jump seat with my Spanish pocket dictionary open. Juan steadily picked up more English phrases, and we all learned a little more colloquial Español (some of which was yelled out by angry motorists and probably not fit for general use).

From this experience we learned that our words may differ but they do not have to keep us imprisoned in tight separate compartments if we really want to seek genuine communication as members of the human family.

Sometimes, I have learned, words are secondary when it concerns communication.

There is a "language" of the hug, the handshake, the smile, the tear—and this sometimes is a better means of connection than all the nouns and verbs in the dictionary.

My first visit to *Yad Vashem* in Jerusalem was traumatic. A visitor enters the large Holocaust memorial knowing what is there but still not exactly sure of what to expect—and one exits in tearful, stunned silence.

Shuffling along with us in the half-darkness were hundreds of visitors from various lands. I heard one or two languages I readily recognized. Others seemed strange-sounding and guttural to my Western ears. Asians.

Africans. Latin Americans. North Americans of all shapes and hues and dress. Teenagers barely dressed in "acceptable" *Yad Vashem* attire. European and Middle Eastern Orthodox Jews in heavy, somber black. All of us moved along the well-marked pathway at a snail's pace, to the accompaniment of sad orchestral music over the sound system.

Shortly after we entered, most of the whispering died out and silence took command. It was that way until we exited an hour later into the bright noonday sunlight.

I looked for the first time at some of my fellow pilgrims. Almost every one was crying. We wept for those who were the victims of Hitler's madness and humanity's apathy. And we were brothers and sisters under *Yahweh* for just a moment—all of us people with common blood ties, created to love and not to hate, to build and not to destroy, to cherish life and not to snuff it out.

Our *dictionaries* were different; the tears, hopes, fears, joys—these made up the powerful common bond we felt that one June afternoon.

◆   ◆   ◆

"Why won't these people speak English?"

The frustrated tourist sharing the limo ride with me from downtown Paris to Charles DeGaulle airport was repeating the common American complaint about the so-called linguistic "rudeness" of the French.

I didn't reply because it would have done little to change his view. We all acquire certain impressions of other cultures; and reason and experience seldom counter those stereotypes. I wanted to tell him of the friendliness I had experienced all across the land…about French students struggling with their English to communicate with me…of my conversation with a small-town parish pastor who had exactly the same challenges I remembered from my own rural pastorate…of taxi drivers offering their advice without expecting an extra tip…and about the young couple who invited me to join the parade and help them celebrate their wedding day.

But I really wanted to tell this fellow American about something *larger* that I have experienced. I would call it the "Pentecost experience". It is a oneness that crosses all boundaries. It is visible in a global community speaking the common language of faith, hope and love. I carry its "dictionary" with me all the time. It opens with *Genesis* and concludes with *Revelation*.

14

Real

"We declare to you...what we have heard, what we have seen with our eyes, what we have looked at and touched with our hands, concerning the word of life."

—(1 John 1:1a)

"Come Visit the *Real Mexico* (or *Canada*, or *China*, or *Florida*)!"

Choose *any* locale in the world and the tourism industry would have us believe that a traveler can—with enough time and money—get to know everything about the land and its people.

But it's not all that easy to get inside another culture and hear its heartbeat.

Sami, our energetic young Palestinian guide in Israel, finally spoke what was on his mind after spending several days mechanically showing us ruins, restaurants and souvenir shops:

"Why don't you Christians come here and spend a little time visiting our homes and worship with us in our own churches? Why do you just want to go to museums and see things from the past?"

After he caught our attention with those words, Sami went on to preach a sermon of sorts as we huddled on a windy, cold Mount of Olives, looking out toward the ancient walls of Jerusalem.

"You know," he said, "we are *people*, we're flesh-and-blood, we have homes and we go to work and we go to church and school just as you do. I would like you to visit the real Palestinian community, see where I live, meet my father."

The invitation was appealing, but the day was about gone and the itinerary had been tightly planned. Besides, our group already had "seen"

Sami's apartment from a distance as we sped through East Jerusalem in our air-conditioned coach.

Like so many other spiritually hungry pilgrims, I had come to Israel and Palestine as before with Bible in one hand and camera in the other to "see the Holy Land". But Sami—as one of the people of the land itself—knew that such a programmed tourist-eye view would offer incomplete and possibly even misleading results.

Sami hoped to prod us to move beyond the sights and sounds of the usual packaged Bible lands "guidebook" journey. He wanted his band of visitors to see more than crumbling walls and dusty archeological excavations, to hear some sounds beyond mournful chanting and lilting calls to prayer…and he hoped to push us on past the constant sight of young soldiers with rifles and children begging to show their stock of olive wood carvings.

"There is a *real* Palestine," Sami kept saying. "This is what I want to tell you about."

Unfortunately, the "real" picture of any nation is something that may differ sharply from the more benign, polished image governments put on display.

Sami, as a member of the shrinking Palestinian Christian community, wanted to show his people in their best light, of course. That's why he would frequently offer impassioned excuses for any lack of basic sanitation and an absence of effusive courtesy in the streets of Arab-dominated communities.

The truth is that most of us who had traveled before and had encountered *reality* here (or in any other land, for that matter) were not all that enamored with it! Much to be preferred were those slick, guidebook perspectives on any country or people—bright pictures without any smudges.

When visitors come to my city, I show them the highlights in keeping with my own prejudiced perspective. Isn't that normal for any proud citizen anywhere? We tend to avoid certain parts of town, look for more famous or spectacular sites, and take time showing off the attractive scenery.

Sami and I are probably much alike in regard to the home turf we love. On one hand, we're a bit vain and don't want guests to know *everything*. We'll often let others have just a peek of "home" as if it were a Hollywood movie set, with exquisite painted scenery in the foreground—while the bare two-by-fours and ragged plastic sheeting are hidden behind the façade.

It's human nature to want to put our best foot forward. But we also ought to help outsiders get a reasonably *accurate* picture of life and people in other lands.

My love for the Holy Land has deepened because I have seen the "real" people of the Book and the "real places" where they were born and likely will live out their days.

Bible lands are not nearly as pretty and pristine as I recall from those copies of nineteenth century etchings that Sunday school teachers used to project on the white wall of our classroom. But it's gratifying to realize that these scenes painted today in the starkness of real life hues are populated with flesh-and-blood persons whose DNA and spiritual nature both are close to my own—and I stand again in awe of the Creator God who brought all this into being!

Too much in life is make-believe—what we would *like* to see rather than what *is*.

And reality offers *its* challenges! I remember the news story of a parent who sued a large theme park because one of its paid actors portraying a comic book character took off his costume for a moment in order to have a needed break. In doffing his costume, he became just an "ordinary person like others"—and the child (so the parent claimed) was "emotionally damaged" because a precious image had been shattered.

Seeing people and places and events in the light of *reality* will at times turn our thinking upside down and shatter stereotypes that we cherish. But the liberation that results from seeking, finding and exploring what is *real* offers an exhilaration and enlightenment beyond price.

15

Guide

"By the tender mercy of our God, the dawn from on high will break upon us…to guide our feet into the way of peace."
—(Luke 1:78–79)

The stocky, tow-headed escort quietly backed himself into a darkened niche near the entrance to the hotel bar. Our visiting American delegation was using the only "gathering room" made available to our integrated group in Johannesburg, South Africa. We knew we were fortunate to be able to snag a few minutes of Desmond Tutu's time—even if we had to accept an unorthodox venue!

Apartheid—the government's identification of racial backgrounds and the ugly discrimination that it served—was still in force, although beginning to lose its grip. Bishop (later to be Archbishop) Tutu, a black Anglican leader, was a leading voice for liberation. And, as we soon discovered, he was watched constantly!

Our so-called "guide" was a fake, as Bishop Tutu humorously disclosed when we sat down and the natty, wiry little cleric stood next to the long oak bar and began to chat informally about conditions in South Africa.

"Meet Mr. Blanck," Bishop Tutu said, pointing to the corner of the room where our "guide" was positioned. "I know you are spying for the government. And I want you to be comfortable. You don't have to stand there all evening—come join us. Tell us what information you need."

A laughing "Mr. Blanck" saluted us with an exaggerated motion and slipped out the door. Our experience that day gave us a practical view of the "problem" in South Africa. It was an object lesson to accompany Bishop Tutu's informal message (which was, in actuality, a word of hope,

45

an accurate prediction that the whole system of injustice in that beautiful but tragic land would soon come crashing down).

Guides. They come in all varieties. Mr. B in Johannesburg was of the rare "kept" variety. He was there through the pleasure of some government bureaucrat, and his mission was to keep tight rein on the foreigners in his company and to make sure they (a) saw the brightest possible picture of things and (b) did not ask too many embarrassing questions about freedom of speech or the status of the nation's underclasses.

The lesson to me from the very beginning of my touring experience was this: *there are good and helpful guides, and there are those one needs to watch out for!* And this is the story of life—the message of faith. Jesus spoke of the "blind guides" who promise to lead people aright but direct them toward moral and spiritual dead-ends.

Walter S. was a very, *very* anti-communist West German who used every opportunity to vilify those from the East who were "ruining" his beloved nation. But Walter reserved his strongest language to speak of those he believed had turned the famed Passion Play at Oberammergau into a commercial marketplace. After the morning performance of the play, Walter stormed out and—in the same spirit Jesus is said to have confronted the temple money-changers—belabored the more aggressive shopkeepers.

"One of these days," Walter grumbled, "I expect to see you people turn the play itself into one great advertisement. Even Pilate will look at Jesus and say, 'Let me find you a nice hand-carved Bavarian cross at a bargain price instead of that crude one the Romans have made.'"

Guides are all too human, I learned. Some would talk with us late at night (after they had imbibed enough wine or beer) about marital problems, family squabbles and government pressures. I learned to empathize with them and be more forgiving of their failings.

Eduardo in Guatemala was the worst guide I had experienced. He didn't talk to us. He slouched in the front seat, staring out the window of the small van we had rented for the day. I fired him on the spot and asked that he get us another guide for the return trip.

The next day, the hotel manager asked me if I knew that Eduardo's brother had been kidnapped two days earlier by some bandits.

What can anyone say in such a situation that will make amends or ease the other's deep grief?

Good guides all seem to have one special knack: even the most inadequate ones always manage to leave their group with at least one serendipitous experience—something unplanned, unexpected and memorable.

I have always reminded tour participants to expect some wonderful surprise along the way—an invitation to tea in an Israeli or Palestinian home, perhaps…a colorful festival under way in a small German village…a new bride and groom posing at the Kremlin…a beautiful little Chinese girl hopping up on a Ming Dynasty stone lion just in time for us to capture her picture.

Good tour guides want the best for each of us. And over the years they have helped me see more clearly the biblical picture of a *Supreme Guide* who leads us through life's challenging terrain toward a destination of peace, joy and purpose.

One of my most memorable "guides", I believe, was not accredited. He was about 15 or 16 and spoke little English. Everywhere we went in the slum outside Rio de Janeiro, he followed us—sometimes pointing out a sight he thought we should note in our journals, often just standing alongside us and smiling a big toothy grin. It was a grim two-hour walk through the *favela* where typical housing was a tin shelter and the sewage system was the smelly stream flowing down the middle of the street. But this was his "home" and he wanted us to see it. At times our eyes had tears, wondering how people such as this youngster could live that way.

When we left we asked our unofficial guide, "What is your name?"

"Jesús," he said. "My name is Jesús."

We returned to our comfortable hotel rooms knowing who had *really* been at our side that whole morning!

16

Value

"...the ordinances of the Lord are true and righteous alto-
gether. More to be desired are they than gold, even much fine
gold."

—(Psalm 19:9b–10a)

Gold and *God* seem to appear together quite often in the story of human-kind.

Our *Museo del Oro* docent in Bogotá, Colombia—well practiced in her craft—dramatically ordered us to close our eyes as we were ushered into a darkened vault-like room.

When the lights were turned on, we found ourselves surrounded by a dazzling array of some 30,000 golden objects. We were looking at treasure created by ancient Indian artisans in tribute to their various deities and rulers. And we also were seeing the golden lure that drew sixteenth-century Spanish warriors and priests to the New World—all in the name of heaven.

As a rather consistent standard of value, gold has always had a close tie to religion, both sophisticated and primitive. Men and women looking for a visible, dramatic way to express commitment to a particular deity or form of worship have turned to that most beautiful and desired metal of the ages. Biblical references to gold abound—whether it be in detailing the fashioning of the Ark of the Covenant or noting the first gift offered to the infant Jesus at Bethlehem.

While plainness and stark simplicity are often seen by many people of faith as especially virtuous, cannot all of us be glad for the golden tributes to divine authority that still enrich our culture and please eyes and hearts generation after generation?

Standing in the ancient cathedral in Toledo, Spain, tourists have to marvel at the dedication of artisan families working across several centuries to produce the great golden altar screens and the many beautiful crosses and symbols that grace this architectural masterpiece.

Golden altars, vases, frames, candlesticks, crucifixes, relic cases, tomb markers, reading stands.

For me the message remains clear: Faith has been important enough to some people across the centuries that they felt compelled to demonstrate its worth by using the world's most recognizable symbol of ultimate value.

Will forthcoming generations make this same judgment about spiritual things?

A legal decision coming out of America's midwest heartland in the 1990's offered a message that seemed quite the opposite. A large financial commitment had been made to a church organization by one of its long-time supporters. When the man died, family members challenged this gift. The court at first overruled the benefactor's wishes, saying that the bequest to a religious organization did "not obtain anything of substantial value". On reflection, the court changed its mind and agreed that the church, indeed, *is* an institution that produces work of "substantial value"!

Measured by secular dollars-and-cents standards, religious concerns may always appear to be impractical, costly, even less than worthy—certainly far from qualifying as a part of modern life fit to stand up and compete for loyalty alongside the glittering "golden" world of commerce, arts, sports, and politics. But I have learned that the ancients were right. Religious faith remains a commodity of immense value, age after age.

How do we judge "value" in today's world? By all of the common tests, matters of soul and spirit attain a high ranking. My friend Bill tells of his uncle Buck, who ran a furniture store in a small southern Indiana town in the early 1940s. When victory was won, Buck was the first to learn about some wonderful new postwar product called the electric refrigerator! He ordered all he could get, but business was at first slow. So Buck—as a good salesman—invited people to trade in their old oak iceboxes and he would give them some credit on their purchase of an electric cooler.

The campaign was so successful that Uncle Buck soon had hundreds of the beautiful hand-made polished oak boxes sitting on a lot behind his store. Unable to get rid of them or to find some immediate use for them, he finally ordered the whole lot burned.

Looking at it from today's perspective, Uncle Buck most certainly destroyed several thousand dollars worth of prized antiques! Those beautiful oak iceboxes became scarce and are still sought after as precious collector's items.

It isn't always easy to determine the ultimate value of a *physical object,* so one can understand how difficult it is at times to assess the true value of what is represented in religious claims and practices. Sometimes the "golden" nature of faith takes a lifetime to discover.

My discovery is that spiritual truth remains deep and durable while other "truth" continues to be a constantly moving target! Religion, as seen in its highest and most noble forms, is concerned with passing along a wisdom that does not change with the wind currents. Biblical faith concerns who we are as persons, affirming our God-derived worth in an impersonal and often uncaring universe.

One test of "value" is that an item or idea must gain in worth over time. Certainly, the basic tenets of religious faith have met that challenge again and again. While institutional religious forms and rituals and methods of telling "the story" change with the years and continue to be shaped and reshaped by fresh discoveries, the foundation holds firm.

Somehow the family artisans who worked for over eight consecutive centuries to complete a solitary golden altar in one Spanish cathedral knew that there was no rush. They would do their very best that day—and then pass the torch along to another generation tomorrow. After all, they knew they were working with God on a project so great that it could never be measured with a mere price tag!

17

Judgment

"Just as it was in the days of Noah, so too it will be in the days of the Son of Man."

—**(Luke 17:26)**

The summer of 1993 was not exactly the best time to schedule a church assembly in St. Louis!

Torrential rains descended on the midwest in May and continued on and on through early September—until St. Louisans and those in adjoining Illinois communities wondered if the mighty Mississippi would soon cover everything and the famed downtown Gateway Arch might be the only safe haven from the rising waters.

Going forward in faith (or because delegates did not want to lose their substantial deposits), two denominations continued plans to hold a joint assembly in downtown St. Louis.

Happily, the waters receded, the infrastructure of the area was restored to normal chaos, and church folks came together for business and prayer without needing life preservers!

On the second day of the assembly, as delegates were moving between business and inspirational sessions, a bearded young man bounded up the steps of the stage and took the podium, microphone in hand. Two or three minutes into his loud and exuberant "address", those milling around the hall suddenly quieted. People realized that this was an *unplanned* speech. The young man was right off the street and definitely not "one of us". The truth was even more apparent when he pulled out his very large King James Bible and started intoning the stern words of *Luke 17* about sin, Noah and the flood!

The church folks were kind to the brash intruder. Two or three very large men put their arms around him and gently but firmly escorted him to the exit.

Sometimes the Bible's heavy emphasis on sin, punishment and salvation *is* a bit more than we want to handle. It's easier to talk about the first part of the equation—the *rules,* the firmness of *the law,* the clear *"thus saith the Lord"* part of faith.

But many find it disturbing—and perhaps unnecessary—to hear a lot of preaching on the "judgment" teachings of faith. We know we need rules, of course, but people ask if they are really that important if God just waves off our foibles and failures and cancels any punishment.

My colleague, Herb, is a biblical scholar whom I respect. If I ever have a question about when or why some portion of Scripture was written or placed in the canon, Herb is my first contact! And he is quick to tell me that he has a special love for the "law" portion of the *Book.*

"I love *Psalm 119* with its tribute to rules and duties," Herb says. "For the writer, God's law was a blessing, not a curse—and this is the way the Apostle Paul also seems to view it."

Human beings, who fundamentally are self-centered and hesitant to take advice or criticism, often need a well-defined framework within which to make decisions and to relate to one another. I find that I need traffic signs and stoplights and a large book of driving regulations to keep me from doing mayhem on the roadway. And I know that I need some clear *moral* rules and signs to keep me on track.

Acceptance of a "divine law"—however one may define it—is necessary and beneficial. And this is what the young bearded evangelist was reminding us in the midst of our Noah-like flood of '93. It just might be as he proclaimed—that God is really dumping the heavens on us because of our rebelliousness. Could God, perhaps, be concerned with the homeless that *we* forget—the poor whom we allow to sleep on downtown streets near multi-million-dollar stadiums? Could the Lord be a bit sour on us because we have forgotten to care for the least and the lost?

I was one who didn't exactly appreciate this odd prophet's harangue during the Great Flood. I needed a sandwich instead of a bombastic lecture on sin and judgment. But I listened—and maybe I learned quite a bit in the process.

I still trust in law. But I love the other part of the story. I also cherish and welcome God's forgiveness and mercy. That makes the law palatable, reasonable and necessary. We try to live by rules but aren't condemned forever when we fail, as we all do at times.

My one experience on a jury involved the trial of an African American man who took a two-by-four from his car trunk and bashed the daylights out of a fellow's windshield.

The law was clear. The perpertrator deserved some punishment for his seemingly senseless act of aggression.

But...in the course of the trial we learned that the man committing this "crime" acted only after he had been shut out—time after time—as he tried to edge his car into a long line of traffic merging into a busy thoroughfare. When the defendant would see a slight opening and pull forward, this one fellow would laugh and tease him and then inch ahead just enough to close the space. After suffering through several minutes of this meanness, the defendant opened his trunk, took out the piece of wood, and took out his frustration on the windshield.

The law said "Guilty as charged!" Love said "You ought to be forgiven and set free!" We the people made the latter decision, and all of us on the jury were pleased with what we had done. Even the prosecuting attorney smiled and nodded our way.

This is why we have laws. We then can appreciate it all the more when someone says to us, "*You* are forgiven. Go and sin no more!"

We may not learn our lesson the first or second or third time, but over the course of a lifetime the message finally gets through. The murky, marring floods of sin come. But so do the rainbows and the cleansing tide of grace!

18

Healing

"Bless the Lord, O my soul, and do not forget all his bene-fits—who forgives all your iniquity, who heals all your dis-eases...."

—(Psalm 103:2–3)

Until I visited Deschapelles, Haiti, and met Larry and Gwen Mellon, I didn't know what *kwashiorkor* was, let alone how to spell it!

But on my first trip to the Mellons' Albert Schweitzer Hospital—a miserable day's drive over deep-rutted roads north of Port-au-Prince—I met one tiny victim of this common tropical illness. And that initial sight of a pot-bellied, reddish-haired infant with matchstick-thin arms and legs is forever seared into my mind and heart.

"You know, this ailment is readily cured," Dr. Mellon sighed. "It's caused by a lack of proper nutrition. We do our best to teach people here the correct habits, but the problem is the awful poverty and the decades of misinformation."

In a few days the little victim of malnutrition probably would look more like a three-year-old should. But she would be returning to her dirt-floored, windowless hut where there was no running water or sanitation. The hospital staff would most likely see her again in a few months. Or perhaps she would be one more of the nameless Haitian poor to be buried with a pseudo-Catholic voodoo "blessing" in one of the hundreds of colorful public cemeteries.

W. Larrimer and Gweldolyn Grant Mellon—born into wealth and security—answered an irresistible call to become healers in the Western Hemisphere's poorest, most desperate and backward little island nation!

What a challenge the Mellons took on in the 1950s when they cashed in most of their personal resources and came to Haiti to build and run a medical mission!

Keeping their work alive for more than four decades became a monumental achievement, considering the economic and political disarray that marked Haitian affairs during the second half of the twentieth century. Whatever success they achieved (and passed on as an enduring legacy) was due to stubbornness, an incredible optimism, and their amazing ability to take a few dollars and multiply them many-fold without surrendering a large number of bribes to the ruling oligarchy in Port-au-Prince.

My recollection of the Mellons is one of simple hands-on compassion, more even than the requisite medical expertise, political savvy and community development skills.

Did this closely-knit team really "accomplish anything" of a permanent nature as far as changing Haitian society? Probably not. After my first visit to this desperately poor little nation I asked the title question in an article: "What Hope for Haiti?" My sad conclusion was that there was *very little*! And I saw that there was not much that the Mellons could do to turn the tide, even with their medical resources and their round-the-clock labors.

I returned several times in succeeding years to the Artibonite Valley and to the starkly simple but beautiful stone complex the Mellons built on the grounds of the old United Fruit Company.

Each time one could see how the strikingly handsome Larry and Gwen both had aged perceptively but also note that their old enthusiasm and energy remained high. They complained about lack of change in Haitian society and about the continuing absence of preventive medicine available to the common people. But they went on with their rigorous daily routine as always. The last time I saw them, it was just a few months before their retirement and too-early passing—and both were tending another fragile child from a remote village who was brought in with *kwashiorkor*!

What is it that drives such men and women of medicine to make a career in out-of-the-way places where there is little financial or professional reward?

The Mellons were compelled by their quiet faith in the Great Physician to go into one of the neediest areas of world and do what they could to ease the hurt of God's children.

This is one of the powerful ways that Christianity has impacted society over the centuries. Followers of Jesus, heeding their Master's call to love and to serve the dispossessed and hurting, have been ones to hold the little brittle-haired, smelly, sickly *kwashiorkor* (or leprosy or HIV or war-wound) victims in their arms and tell them they are not unimportant statistics. Everyone is precious to the One who has given us life.

In so many place of the world the followers of Jesus Christ continue to be healers because they believe that life itself is a divine gift and must be guarded and nurtured.

◆   ◆   ◆

One of the smartest friends I had in high school became one of the brightest and best physicians I ever knew. It was inevitable that Jack would be a general practitioner. You could visualize the stethoscope around his neck when you stood next to him in science class and saw how easily he mastered every assignment!

Jack always seemed to be a bright fellow but a pragmatist with luke-warm religious sentiments. What a surprise it was to visit with him later in life and to learn that he had been spending part of his early retirement time as a lay preacher!

"I think more and more about this wonderful creation called the human body," he said, "and I talk to people about how they can take care of this gift and help others live to the fullest."

Medical men and women called to a "mission".

I still meet them everywhere. Sometimes God sends them out to minister in little-known places of extreme need where even a small band-aid and some iodine work wonders. Most of the time, I see how God plants them down right in the midst of my own community where big miracles of medicine and science are to be seen every day but a gentle human touch and an unexpected word of encouragement are in short supply.

19

Song

"'The Lord is my strength and my song....this is my God, and I will praise him....'"

—(Exodus 15:2a)

In closing their rousing concert of Swahili, English and Afrikaans tunes, the men's quartet from a neighboring black township offered us their version of the African American spiritual, "Down by the River Side".

Our group from the United States clapped warmly along with others of the interracial audience packed tightly into a small block church in *Soweto*. We were, for this one evening, permitted to visit the infamous area outside Johannesburg that derived its ominous "nickname" from its official designation as the *Southwest Township*.

For two or more hours we forgot about the ugly news reports detailing the ongoing troubles in this impoverished, rigidly segregated community. Soweto was home to thousands of black families who were dependent on work in adjoining white communities. The mass migration by bus and train each morning was of biblical proportions. The homecoming each night was marked by the extremes of hymn singing and alcohol-fueled violence. It was marked with a joyous sense of momentary liberation and also the awareness of being watched and threatened by well-armed government police and unofficial militia.

Our presence in Soweto was seen by all of us, visitors and locals, as a small but meaningful witness to international Christian solidarity in the struggle against oppression. We left that night at curfew time, returning to our five-star hotel in the city, feeling good about the encounter, still humming a line of that old spiritual: "Ain't goin' to study war no more, no more...."

The next day, just before lunch, we received word that the young, animated tenor member of the quartet had been waylaid and murdered on his way home from the performance in Soweto. In my heart I still can see and hear and weep for that expressive young singer and his quartet while gladly celebrating the gains in human rights that have come during the three decades since that terrible night.

The music of faith—welling up from the heart and soul—has always had power for particular moments in history, but it also continues to state its message in different ways to different circumstances. So much rich, evocative music emerging from struggle and pain keeps on blessing one generation after another.

Moses and the Israelites sang, as we are told in *Exodus*, "The Lord is my strength and my might". Another word for "*might*" is used as an alternate translation—the word "*song*". To the young tenor in Soweto, expressing through his music the glad conviction that warfare and violence will be "no more" in God's coming realm—*song* was indeed *might*. Music was his daily shield, his constant reminder of God's providence. When a laborer's speech might fail him...when the blaring, angry daily headlines said otherwise...when roaming assassins lurked at every turn with burning rubber tires to immolate any brash dissenter...he could still lift his voice to sing God's praise and celebrate a vision of the victory of love over hatred.

◆   ◆   ◆

My first connection with the church was through song. We in the junior choir dressed in starched white robes and marched down the center aisle of Third Christian Church with the "big choir" right on our heels. We all belted out "Holy, Holy, Holy" as loud as we could, trying to keep up with the volume and pace set by Mrs. Connor at the monstrous pipe organ.

Whenever we learned a new hymn or spiritual, our director, Mrs. Parris, would take time to tell us a bit of its history and discuss (in kid-friendly terms, of course) the song's basic theology.

Music did have power, we discovered as the years moved on. We might not remember what Sunday school teachers taught or what preachers preached, but those great tunes of faith kept running through our minds.

Others share similar experiences with the rich and varied chorales and choruses of faith. At a women's meeting one national church leader told of a happy conversation she had with her son, who was away doing graduate work on a large state campus. The son, who had distanced himself from spiritual concerns, said that he had attended a recent funeral. As the choir and congregation sang Ralph Vaughn Williams' majestic "For All the Saints," he let the tears flow as he recalled the times he had sung it in church. He told his mother how he had been overcome by a powerful sense of God's presence. Through this hymn he came to realize how much he missed the church fellowship in his daily life.

We "sing to the Lord" in many different forms and styles. Those who know the history of church music smile when some tout the "newness" of contemporary praise music, recalling that there have been many such free-wheeling, exuberant, "simple" forms of music used in worship across the centuries.

Our songs may be one-liners with basic beats repeated over and over, or they may be complex tunes with deep, poetic lyrics pushing us to explore the depths of our consciousness and the failings of our unredeemed culture. The richness of hymnody and "religious" music in general will always be something to celebrate.

Music will always be a large part of the way I understand God and offer praise to the One who gives us this gift of song. I will never forget the time I sat around a youth campfire and rejoiced that I could, without fear, "lay down my burden....down by the river side"—and surely I will always remember how those same words were sung with special emphasis by some African men who knew God eventually would make the promise of the old slave tune come true.

20

Courage

"...as you know, we had courage in our God to declare to you the gospel of God in spite of great opposition."

—**(1 Thessalonians 2:2b)**

No one in the State Department said we *couldn't* visit Cuba! Washington officials simply set a few extra hurdles in our path and said if we really wanted to reach Havana, we would have to jump over them.

We considered this shrug-of-the-shoulders attitude as luke-warm permission to make our fraternal church visit to the island for an up-close view of life and religious liberty under the durable Castro regime. So, by way of Mexico City, we flew into Havana to take an enlightening (and tightly monitored) tour of the Communist bastion and to experience for ourselves the effect of the United States embargo.

After only a few hours, we began to discount (and tune out) most of the official line we heard in various forms from our zealous hosts. Everyone wanted to paint the brightest picture of conditions under Castro and to shame us as Americans for placing so many tough trade and travel restrictions in front of our people.

It was hard to be unsympathetic regarding the plight of the common folk. One young waiter asked us, with a cynical grin, "Do you think we are going to overthrow our government just because we can't import your toothpaste and toilet paper?"

Our group had to admit that the government's propaganda machine worked well as we sat through smooth presentations by smiling, colorfully-dressed school children and heard passionate testimonials on behalf of Cuba's universal health care system. Several church leaders told us that religious freedom was, contrary to what we might have heard back home, alive and well on the island.

We could have stayed home and have watched a film! Government-hosted visits of this kind are usually sterile and unproductive. But the good thing is that we stayed in places where we could manage some off-limits conversations with ordinary Cuban men and women. And as we kept our eyes and ears open we were blessed with some honest and extraordinary glimpses of Cuban life and thought.

What we saw, behind the heavy veil of propaganda, were snapshots of courage, resourcefulness and simple human kindness. The years of Communist control had regimented Cuban society but had not changed the fundamental character of the people. Faith remained very much alive. Individual initiative and resourcefulness were incredibly high. Joy was evident in ever-present song and dance and laughter. Opposition to government policies, while muted, was still flourishing in many underground settings.

◆   ◆   ◆

It was a perfect time to visit the beautiful campus of a former Protestant seminary on the north shore of the island. Youth from a small Pentecostal denomination were there on the grounds for a weekend conference in conjunction with meetings of adult leaders of their body.

The first thing we realized was that these young people—by openly declaring and celebrating their faith—virtually lost any chance they might have for higher education opportunities. They would bear the stamp of "Christian" and would be shoved to the back of the line as far as employment or political office.

The youth knew there were spies planted in their midst but they still talked openly of their grievances and their hopes. Their evangelical convictions were expressed in warm and fervent prayer and praise. Everyone, it seemed, brought a guitar to the conference and was more than an average musician!

We left reluctantly when our rickety, patched-up VW van came to get us. We were returning to a land boasting of liberty and opportunity—a place where it is easy to be a believer, or a nonbeliever. We hated to leave these wonderful Cuban young people. But somehow we knew they would make it in life, despite the huge obstacles. They had a quality called "courage" that came from a higher authority than Fidel!

◆   ◆   ◆

And *courage* speaks many other languages, I have learned! My visits to China introduced me to another tightly managed society where that scriptural word describes the way a great many people face up to the awesome power of a godlike state.

One of my missionary heroes was a frail Ohio schoolteacher named Minnie Vautrin, who in 1937 stood at the door of her church compound in Nanjing and told the Japanese invaders, "If you want to cross this threshold, you will have to kill me first." The troops of the imperial army, who murdered some 370,000 Chinese during this "Rape of Nanking," backed away when Miss Minnie barked her orders.

Among the women she saved was one who lived to become the mother of a Christian pastor whom I met forty-six years later in that same city. The son was "violated" in a different way by his own cruel leaders. During Mao's terrible Cultural Revolution (1966–76) he was sent away to the rugged mountains of western China to dig latrines, break rocks and "repent" of his Christian devotion.

The son survived and now, after all these years, had come back to Nanjing to take a role of leadership in the vital young church that was developing there.

Where does such *courage* (or *daring*, in another Bible translation) come from? We cannot manufacture it, generate it at will, or purchase it with tons of gold or silver. It is given to a man or woman as a divine gift—the product of faithfulness and sacrifice—the reward for patient prayer, diligent study of the Word, and unceasing acts of lovingkindness.

21

Success

"...forgetting what lies behind, and straining forward to what lies ahead, I press on...."

—**(Philippians 3:13b–14a)**

Editors love "success stories" because readers hunger for them. All of us need encouragement at times, and it's good to learn that people *can* change and plans *do* often work out despite initial setbacks.

Often, though, the most common and popular story lines have to do with *failure.*

An early reporting assignment took me to the dusty, isolated towns of central Mexico. A long-time missionary nurse/midwife—colorful, capable and committed—was about to retire, and it was time to interview her and to learn about her legendary accomplishments.

"My work has been a failure," she confessed on the first evening of our visit. "I've delivered hundreds of babies but haven't made a dent in the poverty and superstition of these people. My life has been wasted!"

How does a writer put *that* into some paragraphs which will please ever-skeptical financial supporters and keep doors open for anyone who might wish to take up the work after the midwife retires?

Telling the truth about life often means facing up to a brutal reality: *There often are more failures on life's journey than true successes.* And how my downhearted missionary friend dealt with her pain is a key that can help all of us find our way as we stumble along.

This nurse felt sorry for herself for about one day! She needed someone to listen to her and show some empathy during her momentary descent into self-pity. When the sun came up the next morning, she was back on her horse, medical bag in hand, ready for the next delivery.

The real story emerging from my visit turned out to be neither of the two I had on my assignment sheet when I arrived. My final article was not a celebration of past achievements nor a lament over recent setbacks. My report to readers back home was centered on this woman's fresh and exciting commitment to do something about the educational needs of the villagers. I was able to outline exciting *next steps* in her career, not catalog *past missteps*!

In his letters the Apostle Paul often wrote frankly about his miscues and misadventures. He was up-front about his physical frailty. He even owned up to his earlier persecution of Jesus' followers. But in one powerful paragraph to the Christians at Philippi he sets the past in perspective. To be sure, he had done bad things and had failed to do enough good things. But the past didn't matter now. He could start again, unfettered by the baggage of earlier failure.

I like "success stories" and still read them eagerly. There are reports almost daily of exciting breakthroughs in medicine and technology. I love to devour rags-to-riches biographies—or hear the story of some plain wallflower from high school who is now the college beauty queen. I always want my school and professional sports teams to be successful and grumble when they fail to get past the playoffs.

"Success" is a grand and beautiful word. But "failure" need not be a terrifying opposite in our vocabulary. From our failures we can bounce back, learn a bit more about ourselves, grow, and even come back stronger than before.

I have found that any comprehensive story about *achievement* needs several chapters. One must have a long-range perspective to see the whole picture.

I knew an outstanding college president who fell victim to fundraising woes and rising costs and departed on a sour note, convinced that his stint at the helm had been less than positive. It was several years—and well into the term of his successor—before faculty and alumni realized that the seeds of support planted by the former leader were producing incredible fruit.

As a religious insider I probably knew of far more failures than successes! Sometimes those in positions of power and influence proved to have more than a common share of "sinfulness" according to biblical definitions! But I saw in each one of these persons and situations some cause for optimism. Pollyanna-ish as it appears, an objective reporter could find good in so many dismal situations by watching people pick themselves up and move on and make abundant amends for their misdeeds.

Sometimes one had to admit that a whole program or plan was expendable. This was the case with an Appalachian mission center that had a mystique endearing itself to donors and to residents of the mountain community it served.

The school had a reason for existence in its early years but had lost a sense of purpose as the public schools improved and roads opened up that part of Appalachia to the outside world. The clock ran out for this school and it was shut down.

The issue was debated long and fiercely: Was the mission project a failure? Had a colossal mistake been made long before?

I met several leaders of commerce, religion, politics, and education who attended that school in their formative years. Without that institution and its generous financial assistance, these individuals might have drifted off into those beautiful but forbidding mountain "hollers" and never been heard of again!

We never can say with finality that any project undertaken in faith and for a high purpose is a "failure". No *person* who honestly tries his or her best and then misses the mark needs bear the "failure" label forever and ever.

A popular St. Louis newspaper columnist boasts that his "church" is not the "usual" kind, which he views as judgmental. He says he is a member of the "Church of the Second Chance". And its story line—*"From Failure to Success"*—*is* the best kind. That's the theme of the Apostle Paul's biography. And it's repeated thousands of times every day!

22

Shelter

"I would hurry to find a shelter for myself from the raging wind and tempest."

—**(Psalm 55:8)**

We knew him as "Jim"—the jovial little man who lived in a remote corner of our big, rambling church basement and spoke very little understandable English.

Jim had a long Slavic name but someone from the immigration office translated it roughly as "Alexander"—and that's how the kids in our youth group came to know him during the early years of World War II.

Housing this mysterious foreigner with no passport and little worldly goods was our first experience with homelessness on a massive scale. We—children of the Great Depression—had seen some of own native citizens wandering from place to place, looking for work and shelter. But Jim was our introduction to the larger "refugee problem" that began to make headlines in those war years and during the peace era that followed.

Jim turned out to be a true participant in the saga social historians call "the American dream". He worked hard in a gear factory, became a U.S. citizen, found a lovely farm girl to be his bride, fathered two children, and purchased a small tract house in the suburbs where he and his young picture-book family could put down deeper and deeper roots. Jim never quite got rid of his heavy accent but people overlooked this fault because of his ever-cheerful personality.

We who grew up in somewhat normal family circumstances, with a roof over our heads and relatively regular meals, hardly understood or appreciated what it meant to be securely sheltered from life's devastating storms.

People like Jim helped us catch a glimpse of the way a majority of the world's people really live—as helpless, rootless wanderers, dependent on the kindness of strangers or the whim of bureaucrats.

Then there were Alfred and Adolf—the Weiss brothers—who showed us another and more *sinister* dimension to the "refugee crisis", as governments labeled this enlarging global phenomenon.

These young classmates in our elementary school were German Jews who had escaped from Europe and had narrowly missed one of Hitler's death-camp roundups. Bit by bit we heard their frightening personal stories. But our main and more immediate concern may have been the fact that the brilliant Weiss boys were far more advanced in math and science than the rest of us. How could we keep from being a little jealous of these overly bright strangers in our midst?

In small daily personal doses we learned some very large lessons about those whom the Bible calls "strangers and sojourners" of the land. We observed the weightiness of *psychological baggage* these wanderers forever lugged around even when their patched-up suitcases might be nearly empty. We who had shelter (even if rickety and plain) gradually came to view the "problem" of homelessness in a closer and more personal way.

Did our childhood experiences make us any more receptive and kind in the years that followed? Perhaps. At least, as I observed, many of my contemporaries seemed not so quick to brag about their own heritage while devaluing the backgrounds of those who were latecomers among us. Those blessed with shelter of *any* kind and some measure of household security seemed to be among the first to respond to refugee resettlement appeals—the more generous ones who would lead the way in opening doors and putting out a welcome sign when so many were guarded and self-centered.

Statistics seem to show that homelessness in all its many forms increases every year. War, poverty, genocidal "cleansing", ignorance, disease, weather-related crises—all of these issues contribute to a constant upheaval across the earth. Millions continue to be driven from their homes and wander helplessly across the earth.

It was this problem that claimed the minds and hearts of an American mission couple serving in central Africa. Millard and Linda Fuller saw that basic, decent shelter was a primary need if people were to end the cycle of poverty, hunger, failure, and despair. So they began helping the poorest of the poor build simple houses, and that effort—called Habitat for Humanity—took root in the Congo and later became an effective force in the United States and other countries.

Those who travel widely across the world concur that adequate shelter is still one of the most urgent needs of humankind. Half-finished structures dominate the scene in many poorer countries. Slums, ghettoes, resettlement camps, shanty-towns, *favelas*, worker villages—there are so many names to describe all the stinking, crowded, festering places where poor people are forced to live out their days. Changing the environment is not the only answer, to be sure, but the circumstance in which people live is a determining factor in how they view themselves and their worth—and in how they relate to others who are the more fortunate "haves" of the earth.

Our friend Jim was able to escape a life of drudgery, fear and emptiness. The church basement in which he found a temporary home was not the most luxurious of quarters, but it became a clean and hospitable home for a brief time. Having such a modestly secure shelter enabled Jim, the frightened and hopeless refugee, to become "no longer a stranger and sojourner" as the Bible describes it, but a true, valued member of the larger "household"—part of a loving "community" of compassion, faith and mutual respect.

Looking back at simple experiences that shaped my values and deepened my understanding of "good" religion, I can say that no witness was more impressive or lasting than the drama I saw unfold each Sunday in our church basement!

23

One

"Finally, all of you, have unity of spirit, sympathy, love for one another, a tender heart, and a humble mind."

—(1 Peter 3:8)

No one claims to know the names of eye-witnesses or has produced verifiable historical photos, but I tend to believe the story.

As I heard it, a small church in rural Tennessee was the scene of a fierce doctrinal squabble that resulted in bitter division. Long-time residents of the community don't remember the exact point of disagreement, but the lengthy fight split the 100-member congregation down the middle.

Because neither faction had resources to build or buy its own building, the two sides agreed to hold Sunday school and worship in the same frame meeting-place but to set different times.

The nagging problem, though, was a practical one: How would people fuel the old church furnace in winter? Who would pay for the coal used in that era to stoke the fire?

After lengthy study and (one assumes) prayer, elders from both groups agreed that they would have *two* monthly deliveries made. There would be dual coal piles—one designated for each of the factions using the old white frame building.

Relative harmony was maintained for a time. The quiet arrangement seemed to be working. One day, however, embarrassing attention was called to the situation when a wag in the community made a very public observation about the state of faith in the little warring congregation. Where the fading church signboard still proudly advertised "One Lord,

One Faith, One Baptism", a spray painter had added in bold lettering, *"But Two Coal Piles"*.

There is little real humor in the ugly conflict that still separates many people claiming to be children of the same God. My most exhilarating spiritual moments have come in settings where minds and hearts were centered on larger values of faith and life that sincere seekers hold in common. The saddest memories are from times when I witnessed ugly name-calling and saw expressions of prideful arrogance in the name of the Holy One whose way is justice and love.

Unpleasant vignettes still haunt me:

(1) The father of a bride, a good neighbor and an active churchman—kneeling in anticipation at his daughter's interfaith wedding—denied the sacrament and then slapped on the forehead by a clergyman with the stern admonition: "May you see the light!"

(2) An unsmiling fuzzy-cheeked "preacher boy" reacting to my plea for greater understanding among literalists and moderates with the standard argument his great-grandfather used that "it isn't in the Bible so we can't do it".

(3) Churches in formerly hostile societies that struggled to stay alive and proclaim the gospel during repressive years, now using their new freedom and power to deny legitimacy to other dissenting religious groups.

(4) Bible-quoters across the theological spectrum insisting that their political programs and their anointed candidates are the only acceptable options and all who choose otherwise are "ungodly" or lack "true faith".

(5) Astonishingly foolish comments and critiques uttered by those who have no real understanding of others' beliefs but mouth moth-eaten falsehoods and perpetuate false stereotypes.

Happily, scores of positive experiences more than balance the negative ones.

I remember with pleasure the first great international ecumenical gathering I attended as a neophyte religious communicator. Some of us who were impressionable young clergy and laypersons stood in awe as the assembly opened with its seemingly endless, festive parade of religious representatives from across the globe. We saw men and women of all colors and shapes and ages…clergy and laity wearing varied and distinctive garb…some attendees friendly and some regally aloof…leaders with radically differing politics representing widely varied theological camps.

The *beauty* of faith in today's world was—and still is—seen in the rich, enduring and honest diversity of belief and practice. Splendor is found in the adaptability and self-renewing power of faith groups in the face of virulent secularism, and it is evident in the continuing role of healthy religion in resisting the darker ways that lead to the demise of civilization. I celebrate when I see the Spirit pulling people of faith together across so many formidable barriers.

On the other hand, *ugliness* is the only appropriate description of the continuing warfare of words and weapons that mars the religious landscape. The evil face of faith shows in the misuse of our deepest human impulse—*the desire for fellowship with the Source of our being*—as a vehicle to gain and maintain control over others.

One of the central prayers of Jesus was that "they all might be one." Even if that petition does not anticipate or result in uniform belief or totally synchronized action, it does call people who bear the name "Christian" to a life lived in awareness and appreciation of others who are part of the same spiritual household.

Differences in themselves need not trouble us as we look at the large, complex religious scene. We can celebrate the many and varied ways God has spoken to humankind across the centuries. My personal pain comes as I see how believers still create and maintain their separate "coal piles" and cling to the delusion that one can prosper and serve God's purposes by erecting and shoring up the walls that divide and isolate.

Are there visions of unity that draw me into a more hope-filled future? Can God's people some day be one?

I recall conversations with an energetic young minister who stopped by my church office one day to introduce himself and to chat about faith and life. Pastor Rick loves the inner city passionately and wants to reach its people with a message of hope and encouragement in the midst of struggle and change.

Rick and I probably stand at opposite poles theologically, but we found a large common ground on which we could build our friendship. He shamed me with his total childlike trust in God's providential leading, his personal sacrificial lifestyle, and his genuine affection for those victimized by racism and poverty.

"We all need to pray and work together," Pastor Rick told me. "We can't do the job by ourselves. It's too big."

Then my thoughts leap thousands of miles away and I recall some lessons learned on the dusty, dry plains outside Nairobi.

I still cherish that long, hot Sunday spent with one of the new, indigenous African churches of Kenya. What I saw and loved was a vibrant blend of worship style and naively borrowed liturgy that was at first a dazzling bit of "entertainment" for Western outsiders and, finally, a beautiful foretaste of heaven.

We worshipped at the bidding of acolytes dressed in tie-dyed robes and presiding clergy who looked like high Anglican bishops—but were wearing old white sneakers! We sang medleys of African chants, Isaac Watts hymns and Fanny Crosby choruses. Wood and metallic crosses, worn and carried with reverence, had both the Latin shape and the slant-beam Orthodox configuration. Handmade vestments came in rainbow-like colors rather than in traditional hues. Communion wine (available to all) was squeezed from some local fruit-of-the-vine. Women and men—*together*—danced up the aisle with big wicker collection baskets while drums played a rhythmic accompaniment.

After this three-hour service I came away with the feeling that I had been in touch with the universal and eternal church! Was this how one might worship in the heavenly realm?

Another vivid recollection continues to show what God wills for a world that is fractured and in pain. On the final day of an exhausting Holy Land tour, our guide asked if we would like to have a worship service since it was a Sunday and we were visiting several revered Christian sites.

Members of our tour party came from several different faiths. We were Anglicans, nondenominational evangelical Protestants, Pentecostals, Roman Catholics, traditional Baptists, Lutherans. Bring such a group together in one place on a Sunday at home, and few likely could—or *would*—commune with the others.

Think of all the issues: Was a "proper" clergyperson to be in charge of the eucharist? Was there sufficient doctrinal agreement among partakers? Did the blest bread and wine truly become the body and blood of Christ?

As we gathered in the quiet, lush Garden Tomb area, sang a hymn, read from the Gospels, and passed the communion elements to one another, all barriers collapsed. No questions got in the way of our act of remembrance and rededication.

We were, for a glorious moment at least, all one in Christ—all sinners, all receiving tokens of God's amazing grace.

24

More

"And this is my prayer, that your love may overflow more and more with knowledge and full insight...."

—**(Philippians 1:9)**

I scribbled the word *"MORE"* quite often as a beginning journalist.

In the era when news reporters typed their "hard copy" on an old Remington and passed it along to be "marked up" by editors and sent to the typesetters, a writer would want to make sure that no page of the original material was overlooked. So it was standard procedure to note at the bottom of each page the fact that *"MORE"* was to follow. A "30" or a mark similar to the pound sign was used to indicate the end of the piece.

I like *"MORE"* today because it distills the message of the Bible into one small word. In my experience with life and faith, there is never any clear ending point at which we can say that all has been experienced, every task tried and completed (successfully or unsuccessfully), all knowledge acquired, and the final "Amen" said. God always has had something "more" for me to attempt, to discover, to experience, to enjoy.

I can still hear the congregation of my small rural student church singing lustily, "More about Jesus would I know; more of his love to others show." That bouncy old tune was their favorite—and it still reverberates in my soul after many decades. After all these years, I know indeed that there is more Jesus has to teach me...more I can and ought to learn...more blessings awaiting me around the next bend.

Charles Dickens once described an old deacon who would come to church late, sit on the back pew, and promptly go to sleep, not waking until the closing song and benediction. He said that this fellow was absolutely convinced that God had already done everything and had no more plans or revelations—and that was the end of it.

I have refused to live this way but choose the biblical way, which Halford Luccock described as "living on tiptoe". I have kept awake because I do not want to miss anything that God is doing! Living is always exciting because there is so much *"MORE"* to discover about this incredibly wonderful and mysterious universe. There is more wisdom to be gleaned from Scripture; there are more lessons to be passed along by family and friends, more areas for growth of mind and soul.

Another lovely old hymn that I often recall carries the pledge, "More love to thee, O Christ, more love to thee." That is the bottom line on the last page on which I no longer need to write "More" but can put a firm "30" and know that all is done and everything is well—and I am, as promised, in God's sure hands!

978-0-595-39982-6
0-595-39982-7

Printed in the United States
51778LVS00007B/142